Uncover 2  Workbook

Lynne M. Robertson

 CAMBRIDGE UNIVERSITY PRESS

 Discovery EDUCATION

University Printing House, Cambridge CB2 8BS, United Kingdom

One Liberty Plaza, 20th Floor, New York, NY 10006, USA

477 Williamstown Road, Port Melbourne, VIC 3207, Australia

314–321, 3rd Floor, Plot 3, Splendor Forum, Jasola District Centre, New Delhi – 110025, India

103 Penang Road, #05-06/07, Visioncrest Commercial, Singapore 238467

José Abascal, 56–1°, 28003 Madrid, Spain

Cambridge University Press is part of the University of Cambridge.

It furthers the University's mission by disseminating knowledge in the pursuit of education, learning and research at the highest international levels of excellence.

www.cambridge.org
Information on this title: www.cambridge.org/9781107493285

First published 2015

40 39 38 37 36 35 34 33 32 31 30 29 28

Printed in Great Britain by CPI Group (UK) Ltd, Croydon CR0 4YY

A catalog record for this publication is available from the British Library

ISBN 978-1-107-49320-9 Student's Book 2
ISBN 978-1-107-49323-0 Student's Book with Online Workbook and LMS Materials 2
ISBN 978-1-107-49328-5 Workbook with LMS Materials 2
ISBN 978-1-107-49331-5 Teacher's Book 2
ISBN 978-1-107-49338-4 Presentation Plus Disc (DVD-ROM) 2
ISBN 978-1-107-49333-9 Audio CDs 2
ISBN 978-1-107-49335-3 DVD 2

Additional resources for this publication at www.cambridge.org/uncover
Cambridge University Press has no responsibility for the persistence or accuracy of URLs for external or third-party Internet Web sites referred to in this publication and does not guarantee that any content on such Web sites is, or will remain, accurate or appropriate. Information regarding prices, travel timetables, and other factual information given in this work is correct at the time of first printing but Cambridge University Press does not guarantee the accuracy of such information thereafter.

Art direction, book design, layout services, and photo research: QBS Learning

Table of Contents

1 Traditions

Categories

1 Write the letters in the correct categories.

a.	b.
c.	d.
e.	f.
g.	h.
i.	j.
k.	l.

1. music _____ *d* _____, _____

2. sports _____, _____

3. food _____, _____

4. places _____, _____

5. art _____, _____

6. clothing _____, _____

2 Look at the pictures in Exercise 1. Circle the correct answer.

1. Which one is modern?
   d   f   (e)

2. Which one do people wear today?
   a   b   c

3. Which one is a modern place?
   e   g   h

4. Which one is traditional art?
   a   h   j

5. Which one is traditional?
   e   f   l

3 Complete the sentences with the six category words from Exercise 1.

1. My mother won't listen to modern
   _____ *music* _____.

2. They like modern _____ like photography.

3. He sells jeans and T-shirts in a _____ store.

4. She knows how to cook traditional
   _____.

5. You can learn traditional _____ like karate.

6. We like to visit traditional _____ with old buildings.

4 Answer the questions with your own information.

1. What kind of music do you like?
   I like dance music. _____
   Is it traditional or modern?
   _____ *modern* _____

2. What food do you like?
   _____
   Is it traditional or modern?
   _____

3. What clothing do you like?
   _____
   Is it traditional or modern?
   _____

4. What sport do you like?
   _____
   Is it traditional or modern?
   _____

GRAMMAR Simple present review with *be* and *have*

1 Circle the correct simple present forms of *be* and *have*.

1. **A:** Who **is** / (**are**) you?
   B: I **'s** / **'m** Maya's brother.

2. **A:** Where **is** / **are** they?
   B: They **'s** / **'re** at the swimming pool.

3. **A:** What **do** / **does** she **have** / **has**?
   B: She **have** / **has** a laptop. She **don't have** / **doesn't have** a tablet.

4. **A:** When do they **have** / **has** science?
   B: They **have** / **has** science in the afternoon.

5. **A:** **Is** / **Are** he good at soccer?
   B: No, he **isn't** / **aren't**.

6. **A:** **Is** / **Are** we in the same English class?
   B: Yes, we **is** / **are**.

7. **A:** **Do** / **Does** you **have** / **has** a new bike?
   B: No, I **don't** / **doesn't**.

8. **A:** **Do** / **Does** she **have** / **has** traditional clothes?
   B: Yes, she **do** / **does**.

2 Match the questions with the correct answers.

1. Are they in the same class? __*f*__

2. Do you have a bike? _____

3. What's the date today? _____

4. Where are my parents? _____

5. What does he have in his bag? _____

6. Do they have a pet snake? _____

a. They're at the store.

b. He has a tablet. He doesn't have a book.

c. No, they don't. They have a rabbit.

d. It's the 18th.

e. No, I don't. I have a car.

f. Yes, they are.

3 Rewrite the sentences as *Wh-* questions and *yes/no* questions.

1. I am in Ecuador.
   Where are you? / Are you in Ecuador?

2. They are on the football team.
   _____
   _____

3. I have English in the morning.
   _____
   _____

4. She has a new computer.
   _____
   _____

5. He's at the party today.
   _____
   _____

6. They have an old car.
   _____
   _____

4 Complete the questions with *be* or *have*. Then answer the questions with your own information.

1. Where _____*are*_____ you now?
   I'm in the library. _____

2. When do you _____ dinner?
   _____
   _____

3. How old _____ your friend?
   _____
   _____

4. _____ you at the beach now?
   _____
   _____

5. Does your friend _____ a cold?
   _____
   _____

6. _____ it sunny today?
   _____
   _____

1 Put the letters in the correct order to make words.

1. TAH _____*hat*_____

2. NEP _____

3. EHOSS _____

4. SREDS _____

5. HATCW _____

6. CAKTEJ _____

7. OVEENIITSL _____

8. OPHNEELET _____

9. TPOECMUR _____

10. ROHHATGPOP _____

2 Label the pictures with the correct words from Exercise 1.

1. _____*dress*_____

2. _____

3. _____

4. _____

5. _____

6. _____

7. _____

8. _____

9. _____

10. _____

3 Circle the correct answers.

1. Which one is a traditional object?

   a. television

   b. pen

   c. computer

2. Which one is clothing?

   a. photo

   b. phone

   c. dress

3. Which one do people wear on their feet?

   a. phone

   b. shoes

   c. TV

4. Which one DON'T you use to write?

   a. pen

   b. jacket

   c. computer

5. Which one do you wear on your head?

   a. hat

   b. dress

   c. watch

4 Complete the sentences with the correct words.

| pen | phone | photo | ✓TV | watch |

1. They have a new flat screen _____*TV*_____.

2. I have an old black-and-white _____ of my great-grandparents.

3. I use a computer to send emails, but my grandfather uses a _____ to write letters.

4. My mother wears a _____, but I use my phone to tell time.

5. My grandmother sent me a text from her new _____.

GRAMMAR *whose and possessives*

1 Circle the correct answers.

1. (**Whose**) / **Who's** hat is that?

2. **Whose** / **Who's** Alex's sister?

3. **Whose** / **Who's** sister is that?

4. **Whose** / **Who's** are those?

5. **Whose** / **Who's** photos are they?

6. **Whose** / **Who's** on the phone?

2 Complete the chart with the correct possessive adjectives and pronouns.

Possessive adjectives	Possessive pronouns
It's _____*my*_____ phone.	It's mine.
That's your hat.	That hat is _____.
That's _____ photo.	That's hers.
They're his shoes.	They're _____.
They're _____ pens.	They're ours.
It's their TV.	It's _____.

3 Complete the sentences with possessive 's or s'.

1. That's my uncle_'s___ motorcycle.

2. It's my three cousin_____ house.

3. That's my grandparent_____ computer.

4. They're his mother_____ books.

5. It's my parent_____ car.

6. They're the school_____ cameras.

4 Complete the conversation with *whose* and possessives.

Meg: Are these [1]_____*your*_____ photos from your trip?

Robert: Yes, they are. Look. That's my grandparent[2]_____ house. And that's my grandfather[3]_____ new motorcycle.

Meg: Really?

Robert: Yes, it's [4]_____. Look at this photo.

Meg: [5]_____ bicycles are those?

Robert: They're my cousin[6]_____ bikes.

Meg: [7]_____ riding the skateboard?

Robert: That's my mom. It's [8]_____ skateboard.

Meg: Wow! That's cool.

1 **Put the sentences in the correct order to make a conversation.**

	Hiro:	Well, we have a party, of course. But my cousins and I have a new tradition.
	Lena:	That's a cool idea!
	Hiro:	It is. We email it to my grandparents, too. They love it.
	Lena:	Really? How do you do that?
	Hiro:	We use family photos.
	Lena:	That's interesting. What is it?
	Hiro:	We go to the computer lab and make a video.
	Lena:	Tell me about it.
_1_	Hiro:	It's my aunt's birthday on Saturday.

2 **Circle the phrases in Exercise 1 that keep the conversation going.**

3 **Circle the correct answer to keep the conversation going.**

1. **A:** Did you know that brides in India paint their hair red?

   B: a. That's interesting.   b. OK.

2. **A:** I think rock stars are cool.

   B: a. I'm sorry to hear that.   b. Really?

3. **A:** My sister works on TV.

   B: a. Tell me about it.   b. How are you?

4. **A:** I'm in the math competition. We go to Chicago on Monday!

   B: a. See you later.   b. Then what?

4 **Keep the conversations going with the correct phrases.**

| Really? | That's interesting. |
| ✓Tell me about it. | Then what? |

1. **A:** The library has a movie night for teens on Fridays. It's really fun.

   B: *Tell me about it.*

2. **A:** My aunt works at the park. She sees bears a lot.

   B: _____

   A: Yes. There are a lot of bears.

3. **A:** The new mall is open. It has an ice cream shop next to a gym.

   B: _____

4. **A:** There's a band competition in the park on Saturday. My band thinks we can win it.

   B: _____

   A: Then we win some money!

1 Complete the invitation with the correct question words.

| Who | ✓What | Where | When | Why |

Tim's Party!

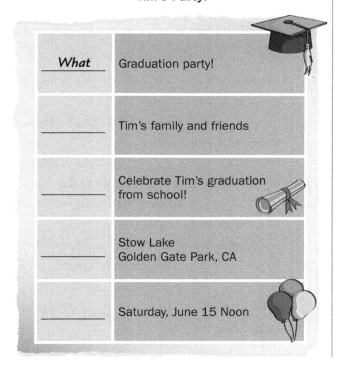

__What__	Graduation party!
_____	Tim's family and friends
_____	Celebrate Tim's graduation from school!
_____	Stow Lake Golden Gate Park, CA
_____	Saturday, June 15 Noon

3 Circle the correct answers.

1. **There is / There are** a lot of people in my family.

2. **There is / There are** many interesting traditions in the world.

3. **There is / There are** a museum with traditional Asian art on Larkin Street.

4. **There is / There are** a new sport called "snow kiting."

5. **There isn't / There aren't** a professional women's baseball team.

4 Write sentences about Tim's party. Use the word web from Exercise 2. Use *There is / There are*.

1. *There is a birthday party for Tim in the park.*

2. _____

   _____

3. _____

   _____

4. _____

   _____

5. _____

   _____

2 Complete the word web with information about Tim's party.

> cake, music
> lots of games, activities
> many friends, grandparents, cousins
> Saturday noon
> ✓the park

When
_____
_____
_____

Where
the park
_____
_____

Tim's graduation party

What
_____
_____

Who
_____
_____
_____

2 What's Playing?

1 Complete the crossword puzzle.

ACROSS   DOWN

3.

1.

6.

2.

7.

4.

8.

5.

9.

2 Complete the paragraph with words from Exercise 1.

My Post

I love movies! I like [1]_____*action*_____ movies the best. They are so exciting. I do karate, so I also like [2]_____ movies to see the kung fu experts. When I want to laugh, I watch a [3]_____ or sometimes an [4]_____ movie, even though they are for kids. My mom likes the love stories in [5]_____ movies so I watch them with her. My dad is very serious, and we watch [6]_____ together. My brother likes special effects, so he watches [7]_____ movies. I don't like to watch [8]_____ movies because I get scared. And I don't like to watch [9]_____, even though the singing is good.

😊   **Comment**

3 Complete the sentences with your own ideas.

1. My favorite type of movie is
   _____*horror movies*_____ because
   _*I like scary stories*_____.

2. The name of my favorite movie is
   _____
   _____.

3. My favorite movie villain is _____
   _____ because
   _____.

4. I don't like _____
   movies because _____
   _____.

5. I never watch _____
   _____.

1 Match the questions with the correct answers.

1. Do you like action movies? __c__

2. Does Helen like romance movies? _____

3. Do they watch "Bollywood" movies? _____

4. What type of movies do you watch? _____

5. Where do they watch movies? _____

6. How often does Maria go to the movies? _____

a. They watch movies at home.

b. Yes, she does.

c. No, I don't.

d. I watch horror movies.

e. She never goes to the movies.

f. Yes, they do.

2 Complete the chart. Use the simple present.

	Questions	Affirmative	Negative
1. I	What movies do you like?	I __like__ musicals.	I __don't like__ dramas.
2. They	What _____ they _____ her?	They call her "J.Lo."	They _____ her Jennifer Muñiz.
3. She	How often _____ Sally _____ to the movies?	She _____ to the movies two times a week.	She doesn't go to the movies on Fridays.
4. I	Do you like documentaries?	Yes, I _____.	No, I _____.
5. They	_____ they watch movies at school?	_____.	_____.
6. He	_____ Owen _____ to the movies?	_____.	_____.

3 Complete the chart with adverbs of frequency.

✓always   never   often   sometimes   usually

_____ *always*

_____

_____

_____

_____

4 Put the words in the correct order to make sentences.

1. watch / at / never / movies / night / horror / I / .

   I never watch horror movies at night.

2. with / I / watch / sisters / my / romance / usually / movies / .

   _____

3. movies / on / her / sometimes / watches / computer / She / .

   _____

4. always / animated / brother / movies / My / on / the / watches / weekends / .

   _____

5 Answer the questions with your own information.

1. How often do you watch movies at school?

   We sometimes watch movies at school.

2. When do you watch movies with your friends?

   _____

3. What types of movies do you never watch?

   _____

4. Where do you usually watch movies?

   _____

5. Do you go to the movie theater? How often?

   _____

VOCABULARY Types of TV shows

1 Find the words for TV shows.

cartoon	crime series	documentary
game show	reality TV show	sitcom
soap opera	talk show	✓ the news

H	T	H	E	N	E	W	S	O	E	N	U	J
R	E	A	L	I	T	Y	T	V	S	H	O	W
R	P	C	A	R	T	O	O	N	S	T	Y	Z
P	C	R	I	M	E	S	E	R	I	E	S	U
E	Z	V	X	H	I	N	R	Y	Z	R	H	G
O	R	Q	E	B	I	P	N	L	V	K	K	T
M	X	D	O	C	U	M	E	N	T	A	R	Y
R	D	K	W	F	O	M	V	E	L	H	P	M
D	S	I	T	C	O	M	K	U	R	S	R	T
J	S	O	A	P	O	P	E	R	A	N	L	W
J	J	N	S	V	P	Y	O	K	Q	E	S	Q
L	G	A	M	E	S	H	O	W	C	R	P	Y
Z	T	H	I	T	A	L	K	S	H	O	W	K

2 Label the pictures with the correct types of TV shows from Exercise 1.

1. _____ *reality TV show* _____

2. _____

3. _____

4. _____

5. _____

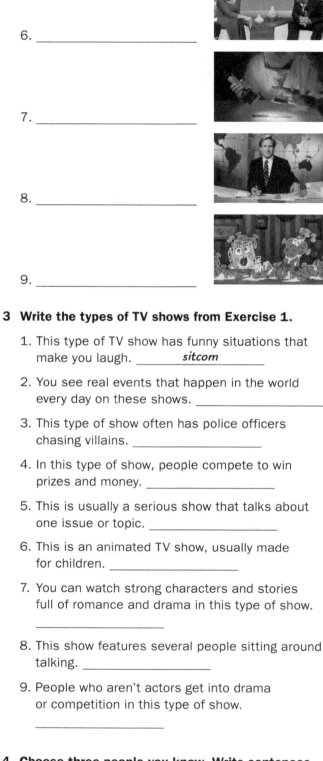

6. _____

7. _____

8. _____

9. _____

3 Write the types of TV shows from Exercise 1.

1. This type of TV show has funny situations that make you laugh. _____ *sitcom* _____

2. You see real events that happen in the world every day on these shows. _____

3. This type of show often has police officers chasing villains. _____

4. In this type of show, people compete to win prizes and money. _____

5. This is usually a serious show that talks about one issue or topic. _____

6. This is an animated TV show, usually made for children. _____

7. You can watch strong characters and stories full of romance and drama in this type of show.

   _____

8. This show features several people sitting around talking. _____

9. People who aren't actors get into drama or competition in this type of show.

   _____

4 Choose three people you know. Write sentences about the TV shows they watch.

1. *My parents watch the news.* _____

2. _____

3. _____

4. _____

5. _____

GRAMMAR Verb + infinitive or -ing form (gerund)

1 Does each sentence have a verb + infinitive or a verb + -ing form (gerund)? Underline verb + infinitive. Circle verb + -ing form.

1. She <u>loves to read</u> comic books. / She (loves reading) comic books.
2. My brother dislikes buying new clothes.
3. Ellen prefers watching movies to reading movie reviews.
4. Henry needs to get money to buy a bike.
5. Mila enjoys watching all types of movies.
6. They want to write a movie script together.

2 Use the phrases to complete the chart with verb + infinitive or verb + -ing form (gerund).

dislikes being	dislikes reading	hates being
hates to be	✓need to see	prefer eating
prefer to eat	wants to go	

Verb + infinitive	
You _____*need to see*_____ this TV show.	
Howie _____ to outer space.	

Verb + -ing form (gerund)	
Sheldon _____ wrong.	
Penny _____ comic books.	

Verb + infinitive or -ing form (gerund)	
Raj _____ shy. / Raj _____ shy.	
They _____ Thai food on Monday night. /	
They _____ Thai food on Monday night.	

3 Correct the sentences.

1. I dislike ~~to go~~ *going* to bed late.
2. They enjoy to washing the dog.
3. We need seeing the map.
4. Helen likes study science at school.
5. Hank wants to watching sports on TV.
6. She hates get up late.

4 Write sentences with your own information. Use *love, enjoy, want, prefer, dislike,* and *hate* plus the infinitive or -ing forms of the verbs in the box.

| get | ✓play | read | study | watch | work |

1. (love) *I love to play video games.*
   I love playing video games.
2. (enjoy) _____
   _____
3. (dislike) _____
   _____
4. (want) _____
   _____
5. (hate) _____
   _____
6. (prefer) _____
   _____

1 Put the words in the correct order to make sentences.

1. do / feel / you / How / about / reality TV shows / ?

   How do you feel about reality TV shows?

2. my / In / they're / opinion, / boring / .

   _____

3. about / you / sitcoms / do / think / What / ?

   _____

4. OK / I / they're / think / .

   _____

5. about / you / soap operas / do / How / feel / ?

   _____

2 Put the sentences in the correct order to make a conversation.

_____ **Paul:** Well, I watch for the story, not the acting.

_____ **Erika:** In my opinion, they're really awful. The actors who play the villains are so bad.

_____ **Paul:** I think they're boring. I prefer to read a book.

_____ **Erika:** Oh, well, then what do you think of documentaries?

_*1*_ **Paul:** Hey, Erika. What do you think about crime series?

_____ **Erika:** I think they're great. You can learn a lot.

3 Ask for and give opinions. Use the phrases and your own opinions.

How do you feel about	In my opinion,
I think	What do you think about

1. *How do you feel about* _____ soap operas?

   _____

   _____

2. _____ crime series?

   _____

   _____

3. _____ reality TV shows?

   _____

   _____

4. _____ sitcoms?

   _____

   _____

1 Read Tim's movie review. Then complete the chart.

This review is of Disney's *Maleficent*. It is an action/ adventure movie based on the villain from the old fairy tale, "Sleeping Beauty." It has the same director as *The Hunger Games*, Robert Stromberg.

Angelina Jolie stars as Maleficent, a beautiful fairy from a long time ago in a peaceful forest. But one day, a human army invades the forest and threatens the peace. Maleficent becomes a strong leader, but someone betrays her so her heart turns to stone. She *curses the human king's new baby, Aurora, to die before she is 16. As the baby grows older, Maleficent learns that Aurora (actor Elle Fanning) may be the key to peace in the forest.

I like this movie because it is a new story about an old villain. Angelina Jolie is beautiful and mysterious as Maleficent, so she makes the character very interesting. The fairy tale really comes to life because the director did a good job with the camerawork and costumes.

*__curse__ – to use magical words that make something bad happen

Main characters and actors	Director Robert Stromberg
Type of movie	Time and place
Short description of the story	
Why you like it or don't like it	

2 Complete the chart about a movie you like.

Main characters and actors	Director
Type of movie	Time and place
Short description of the story	
Why you like it or don't like it	

3 Circle the examples of the connectors *so* and *because* in Exercise 1. Then use your notes from Exercise 2 to write sentences using *so* and *because*.

1. *I liked this movie because the animation looked very real.*

2. _____

_____

3. _____

_____

4. _____

_____

1 Put the words in the correct columns.

| basketball | hip-hop | jazz |
| meat with corn | pizza | sumo wrestling |

Food	Music	Sports

2 Write one traditional thing for each category from Exercise 1.

1. Food: _____

2. Music: _____

3. Sports: _____

3 Complete the questions and answers with the correct forms of *be* or *have*. Then match the questions with the correct answers.

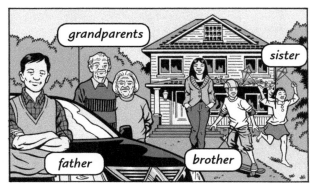

1. What _____ he _____ for lunch? _____

2. How old _____ Ken? _____

3. Do they _____ a tablet? _____

4. _____ they your cousins? _____

a. Yes, they are.

b. He's 15. He _____ 17.

c. He _____ sushi. He doesn't have a burger.

d. No, they don't.

4 Look at the picture. Complete the sentences with the correct possessives.

grandparents

sister

father

brother

1. It's my _____ house.

2. It's my _____ car.

3. It's my _____ skateboard.

4. They're my _____ kites.

5 Rewrite the sentences in Exercise 4 in two different ways. Use possessive adjectives and possessive pronouns.

1. It's _____ house. It's _____.

2. It's _____ car. It's _____.

3. It's _____ skateboard. It's _____.

4. They're _____ kites. They're _____.

6 Complete the sentences with *always*, *usually*, *often*, *sometimes*, or *never*. More than one answer may be possible.

Jean	Michelle	Ella
Watches TV every day from 7:00–9:00 p.m.	Watches TV most Mondays from 4:00–6:00 p.m. and watches movies every other weekend	Watches movies once in a while on Sundays

1. Michelle _____ watches TV on Tuesdays.

2. Jean _____ watches TV from 7:00 to 9:00 p.m.

3. Ella _____ watches movies on Sundays.

4. Michelle _____ watches movies on the weekends.

7 **Rewrite the sentences and questions to make them correct.**

1. When types of movies does your parents likes?

   _____

2. Does they likes comedies?

   _____

3. They doesn't call him Mr. Sparrow.

   _____

4. She teach at my school three times a week.

   _____

8 **Complete the conversation.**

always	so
hate watching	Tell me about it.
horror	That's interesting.
I think	want to watch
need to see	Whose
Really	

Mark: Let's go see *Godzilla* at the theater.

Anna: Maybe. ¹_____

Mark: Well, it's a ²_____
movie about a big monster.

Anna: I dislike those types of movies. I

³_____ a comedy
on TV. *Modern Family* is on tonight.

Mark: ⁴_____? You can

⁵_____ watch TV. But
the movie is only at the theater this week.

Anna: ⁶_____ we can rent
Godzilla and watch it at home.

Mark: I ⁷_____ movies on a

TV! You ⁸_____ horror
movies on a big screen!

Anna: ⁹_____

¹⁰_____ flat screen
TV is it? Don't you have this big TV

¹¹_____ that you can
watch movies?

9 **Answer the questions about your favorite movies and TV shows. Write complete sentences.**

1. What is your favorite movie? What type of movie is it?

   _____

   _____

2. How often do you watch TV?

   _____

   _____

3. What types of movies or TV shows do you dislike? Why do you dislike them?

   _____

   _____

   _____

4. How do you feel about documentaries? Why?

   _____

   _____

   _____

3 Spending Habits

VOCABULARY Places to shop

1 Find 10 more words for places to shop.

| ATM   bank   ✓bookstore   clothing store |
| department store   electronics store |
| food court   jewelry store   music store |
| pharmacy   shoe store   sporting goods store |

T	Z	G	V	U	E	W	U	F	P	G	O	C	X	F	H	N	L	J
A	G	E	L	E	C	T	R	O	N	I	C	S	S	T	O	R	E	Q
Q	Z	A	T	M	W	P	D	J	B	P	M	U	N	N	A	E	J	K
N	M	U	S	I	C	S	T	O	R	E	N	D	P	D	A	F	G	R
D	N	N	D	E	P	A	R	T	M	E	N	T	S	T	O	R	E	A
F	Y	V	L	J	E	W	E	L	R	Y	S	T	O	R	E	N	T	P
B	O	O	K	S	T	O	R	E	X	T	B	A	N	K	Y	R	M	V
F	S	P	O	R	T	I	N	G	G	O	O	D	S	S	T	O	R	E
I	S	H	O	E	S	T	O	R	E	C	P	H	A	R	M	A	C	Y
V	N	W	D	M	I	C	L	O	T	H	I	N	G	S	T	O	R	E
Y	I	Q	M	S	Z	D	L	B	F	O	O	D	C	O	U	R	T	P

2 Put the places from Exercise 1 in the correct columns. Use each word only once.

Where to get . . .			
things you can wear	**things you can play**	**things you need to pay for things**	**many different types of things**
shoe store	___	___	___
___	___	___	___
___			

things you need to be healthy	**things to read**	**things to eat**
___	___	___

3 Where can you do these things? Write places from Exercise 1.

1. My sister bought a new MP3 player at the
   _____electronics store_____.

2. I like to read. I want to go to the
   _____.

3. We can eat lunch at the
   _____.

4. She saw a pretty necklace at the
   _____.

5. They went to the _____
   to buy a new tennis racket.

6. We can find a wedding gift at the
   _____. They sell everything.

7. When my little brother is sick, I buy medicine
   from the _____.

8. I take money out from the
   _____ to go to my
   favorite stores.

4 Complete the sentences with your own information.

1. My favorite type of store is
   a clothing store. I like to buy jeans.

2. I always shop at the
   _____
   _____

3. I never shop at the
   _____
   _____

4. On the weekend, I dislike going to the
   _____
   _____

5. I sometimes go to the
   _____
   _____

16 | Unit 3

GRAMMAR Present continuous review

1 Complete the chart using the present continuous.

Affirmative	Negative
1. I *'m getting* lunch at the café. (get)	I *'m not getting* lunch at the food court.
2. My friend Hal _____ at the bank now. (wait)	He _____ at the electronics store.
3. My teacher _____ at the clothing store today. (shop)	My teacher _____ at the bookstore.
4. My sister _____ a book bag online for school. (buy)	She _____ a backpack at the department store.
5. The class _____ in their notebooks right now. (write)	They _____ on their laptops.

GRAMMAR Simple present vs. present continuous

2 Complete the questions and answers. Use the present continuous or the simple present.

1. What _____ *are* _____ you _____ *watching* _____ right now? (watch)

   I'm watching a movie. I *'m not watching* _____ TV. (not watch)

2. What _____ she _____ today? (do)

   She's not running in a race. She _____ on Mondays. (study)

3. Where _____ they _____ right now? (go)

   They _____ to the beach. (go) They _____ when it's sunny. (not hike)

4. _____ you _____ about a mall in Dubai today? (write)

   Yes, I am. But I usually _____ about shopping malls. (not write)

5. _____ he _____ clothes now? (change)

   No, he's not. He usually _____ his basketball uniform home. (wear)

3 Complete the conversation with the correct forms of the verbs.

✓ are	buy	do	look	study
are	✓do	get	shop	walk

Alana: Hello, Vivian. What ¹_____ *are* _____ you ²_____ *doing* _____?

Vivian: Hi. I ³_____ with my sister, Haley. We ⁴_____ at hats.

Alana: Hats?

Vivian: Well, Haley is. But I'm ⁵_____ a hat. I need to buy sneakers for basketball. ⁶_____ you ⁷_____ your dog outside?

Alana: I wish! I'm ⁸_____ for the science test.

Vivian: Oh, too bad. I hate ⁹_____ homework on the weekend.

Alana: Me, too. But I hate ¹⁰_____ bad grades more.

4 Write sentences about you. Use the present continuous or the simple present.

1. What are you doing right now?

   I'm studying English.

2. Where are you right now?

   _____

3. Do you usually study English at this time?

   _____

4. What are you writing with right now?

   _____

1 Circle the seven money verbs.

s(ave)earnborrowspendlenddepositwithdraw

2 Match each word with its opposite.

1. borrow   a. spend

2. deposit   b. save

3. earn   c. lend

4. spend   d. withdraw

3 Correct the sentences.

withdraws
1. When he needs money, he ~~lends~~ it at the ATM.

2. I earn my allowance by putting it in the bank.

3. My cousin deposits money from me.

4. We work after school to withdraw money to buy a bike.

5. I prefer to borrow my money on concerts, not on clothes.

4 Write sentences describing a good friend or someone in your family. Use the money verbs.

1. (save) _My friend Bill saves his money every month._

2. (earn) _____

_____

3. (deposit) _____

_____

4. (withdraw) _____

_____

5. (spend) _____

_____

6. (borrow) _____

_____

7. (lend) _____

_____

GRAMMAR Quantifiers

1 Circle the correct quantifiers.

1. I don't have **many** / **any** money until Friday.

2. Are there **much** / **many** T-shirts on sale?

3. She's not old **enough** / **some** to babysit.

4. How **a lot of** / **much** time do you have to study tonight?

5. Kevin earns **some** / **any** money selling cookies.

6. They don't have **much** / **a lot of** people on their team.

2 Complete the chart with quantifiers. More than one answer may be possible.

With countable plural nouns
1. How _____*many*_____ sweaters do you have?
2. I have _____ sweaters.
3. I don't have _____ sweaters.
4. Are there _____ sweaters in your closet?

With uncountable nouns
5. How _____*much*_____ money do you save every month?
6. I save _____ money every month.
7. I don't save _____ money every month.
8. Is there _____ money for the trip?

3 Complete the conversation with the correct quantifiers.

any	How many	some
enough	✓How much	

Jackie: The concert tickets are on sale now. Do you want to buy one?

Andrew: I want to buy two. [1] ____*How much*____ is a ticket?

Jackie: They're $25.00 each.

Andrew: Oh no! I don't have [2]_____ money. Can I borrow [3]_____ money?

Jackie: Sorry. I don't have [4]_____ money either. Who is the other ticket for?

Andrew: It's for Erika.

Erika: Andrew! I'll buy our tickets. [5]_____ times do I have to tell you that?!?

4 Complete the questions with quantifiers. Then answer the questions with your own information.

1. How _____*many*_____ tests do you have this week?

   I don't have any tests this week.

2. Are there _____ cafés in your town?

   _____

   _____

3. How _____ time do you spend online every day?

   _____

   _____

4. How _____ students are in your class?

   _____

   _____

5. Do you have _____ time to watch movies on the weekend?

   _____

   _____

6. How _____ times do you text each day?

   _____

   _____

1 Put the words in the correct order to make sentences a shopper might say. Then match the sentences to the responses.

1. like / some / to / sneakers / I'd / buy / .

   I'd like to buy some

   sneakers.   _d_

2. Can / on / try / I / them / ?

   _____

   ____

3. ones / prefer / red / I'd / those / .

   _____

   ____

4. them / I'll / take / !

   _____

   ____

a. The red ones are very nice. Here, try them on.

b. Of course. Here you are.

c. OK. That'll be $39.

d. OK. How about these green ones?

2 Put the sentences in order to make a conversation.

___1___ **Brandon:**   I'd like to buy <u>some sneakers</u>, please.

_____ **Clerk:**   OK. That'll be $59.

_____ **Brandon:**   <u>Good. They're big enough.</u> I'll take them.

_____ **Clerk:**   OK. How <u>about these blue basketball sneakers</u>?

_____ **Brandon:**   Hmm. I'd prefer <u>ones to play basketball in</u>.

_____ **Clerk:**   OK. Try <u>these</u>. How do they fit?

_____ **Brandon:**   <u>Size 11</u>.

_____ **Clerk:**   Of course. What size do you wear?

_____ **Brandon:**   Can I try <u>them</u> on?

_____ **Clerk:**   OK. How about <u>these black ones? They're great for running</u>.

3 Rewrite the conversation in Exercise 2 in order. Change the underlined words to use your own ideas.

1. **You:** I'd like to buy _____, please.

2. **Clerk:** _____

3. **You:** _____

4. **Clerk:** _____

5. **You:** _____

6. **Clerk:** _____

7. **You:** _____

8. **Clerk:** _____

9. **You:** _____

10. **Clerk:** _____

READING TO WRITE

1 Read the review. Label the information with the words and phrases.

| don't like | like | ✓name of product | recommendation | the price | where to buy |

Rain Boots

name of product

[1]Splashy Rain Boots are for sale [2]online. They really keep your feet dry. [3]They come in lots of fun colors, like purple. [4]The price is good, too: only $29. The boots are high enough to step in deep puddles on rainy days. [5]The only problem is that they are too big. I am usually a size 7, but I got these in size 6. [6]When you order them, buy one size smaller!

2 Circle the correct answers.

1. My cell phone is great. **Buy** / **Don't buy** one like mine.

2. **Get** / **Don't get** these T-shirts today. Wait until Saturday and save $10.

3. The hotel is very pleasant. **Spend** / **don't spend** your next vacation here!

4. The fruit at this store is old. **Shop** / **Don't shop** here if you want fresh fruit!

5. These sweaters come in many colors. **Buy** / **Don't buy** more than one if you can.

6. The concert seats aren't very good. Let's **get** / **not get** the tickets.

3 Write recommendations about products you use. Use imperatives.

1. *Don't buy the newest cell phone.*

2. _____

3. _____

4. _____

5. _____

4 Our Heroes

VOCABULARY Cool jobs

1 Use the pictures to complete the crossword.

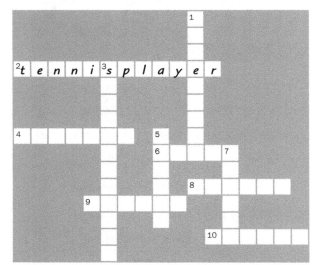

Crossword:
²t e n n i ³s p l a y e r

ACROSS

2.

4.

6.

8.

9.

10.

DOWN

1.

3.

5.

7.

2 Circle the correct answers.

1. Which job is a sports job?

   a. painter   b. writer   ⓒ soccer player

2. Which job is an academic job?

   a. scientist   b. runner   c. singer

3. Which job is a job in the arts?

   a. scientist   b. soccer player   c. writer

4. Which is NOT a job in the arts?

   a. dancer   b. painter   c. runner

3 Write a sentence about a famous person for each of the jobs listed below.

1. scientist *Neil deGrasse Tyson is a famous scientist.*

2. tennis player _____

3. soccer player _____

4. actor _____

5. singer _____

4 Complete the sentences with the jobs from Exercise 1.

○○○

I think a lot about what type of job I would like. I love sports! I'm a ¹ ___*soccer player*___ on the school team. I'm also a ² _____, but I'm not on the team. I just play my brother. I'm not a very fast ³ _____. I like sports, but I don't think I want to do sports as a job.

I don't want to work in arts or entertainment. I'm not good at making pictures, so I don't want to be a ⁴ _____. I don't have a good voice, so I can't be a ⁵ _____. And I don't like to talk in front of an audience, so I don't want to be an ⁶ _____. I'm athletic, but I don't move well, so I can't be a ⁷ _____.

I like rules, but I don't like to argue, so I wouldn't want to be a ⁸ _____. I'm not very good at math or chemistry, so I wouldn't want to be a ⁹ _____. I do like telling stories and reading books, so maybe I could be a ¹⁰ _____. I could work for a sports magazine!

1 Complete the chart with verbs in the simple past.

Affirmative statements	Negative statements
She _____ a millionaire at age 21.	She _____*wasn't*_____ a millionaire at age 20.
I _____*was*_____ in a play a month _____*ago*_____.	I _____ in a movie last month.
He _____ in a restaurant.	He ___*didn't work*___ as a lawyer.
They _____*tried*_____ to play tennis a week _____*ago*_____.	They _____ to play last month.
She _____ a race in 2010.	She ___*didn't run*___ any races in 2014.
We _____*won*_____ the match a year _____.	We _____ the match.

2 Write the correct forms of the verbs.

1. I _____*lived*_____ in São Paulo when I was five. (live)

2. His father _____ in Hong Kong five years ago. (work)

3. They _____ for running shoes last weekend. (shop)

4. We _____ surfing when we were at the beach. (try)

5. She _____ a job with the New York City Ballet. (not get)

6. The band _____ their first video in 2011. (not make)

7. I _____ a job as a singer three months ago. (not have)

8. She _____ a popular book in 2007. (not write)

3 Write statements about Daniella using the simple past. Use information from the chart.

	Affirmative	Negative
1. live	Mexico City	Paris
2. want to be	painter	doctor
3. has	friends	brothers or sisters
4. work	in a library	in a café
5. win	awards	medals

1. *Daniella lived in Mexico City. She didn't* _____
   live in Paris. _____

2. _____
   _____

3. _____
   _____

4. _____
   _____

5. _____
   _____

4 Complete the sentences with the simple past and your own ideas. Write affirmative or negative statements.

1. I ___*was in sixth grade*___ two years ago. (be)
   _____

2. I _____ five years ago. (live)
   _____

3. My friends and I _____ last year. (like)
   _____

4. I _____ last month. (play)
   _____

5. My parents _____ for three years before I was born. (be)
   _____

6. I _____ when I was five. (want to be)
   _____

1 Put the letters in the correct order to make personality words.

1. MALC _____calm_____

2. DIKN _____

3. NUFYN _____

4. EVBAR _____

5. EITUQ _____

6. ROSESIU _____

7. BRSTNUOB _____

8. LEFUCERH _____

9. DREFYLIN _____

2 Match the definitions with the correct words from Exercise 1. Write the number for each.

____5____ doesn't talk a lot

_____ makes you laugh a lot

_____ doesn't get excited

_____ isn't scared of things

_____ is always happy and smiling

_____ likes to meet new people

_____ studies all the time

_____ won't listen to others

_____ helps others and is nice

3 Complete the paragraph with the personality words from Exercise 1. Then write the name of each girl beside the picture.

brave	✓cheerful	funny	kind	serious

My name is Stella. I want to tell you about my friends. First, there's Emily. She is very ¹ _cheerful_ . If you want to have a party, she will make it fun. My friend Tina is very ² _____ . She makes me laugh. My friend Mala is the ³ _____ one. She's not scared of anything. Jane is my nicest friend. She is very ⁴ _____ . Then there's Anna. She studies a lot, so my friends say that she's ⁵ _____ .

_____

_____

_____Emily_____

_____

_____

4 Use the adjectives of personality to write sentences about yourself, your friends, and your family.

1. _My brother is funny._

2. _____

_____

3. _____

_____

4. _____

_____

5. _____

_____

GRAMMAR Simple past questions review and *ago*

1 Match the questions with the correct answers.

1. How was she few minutes ago?	a. It started five minutes ago.
2. Where was she?	b. Yes, I did.
3. Did you see the shark?	c. I called the beach patrol.
4. How long ago did it start following her?	d. She was happy and having fun.
5. Who did you call?	e. She was far from the beach.
6. What did they say?	f. Yes, she was!
7. Was she scared then?	g. They said to wave at her and point to the shark.

2 Complete the questions.

1. What ___*did*___ you ___*do*___ yesterday? (do)

   We went camping.

2. _____ you _____ the fire? (see)

   Yes, we did.

3. Where _____ you when it started? (be)

   We were in the tent.

4. How long ago _____ it _____? (start)

   It started two hours ago.

5. Where _____ you _____? (run)

   We ran up that hill.

6. Where _____ they _____ the campers? (put)

   They put them on the fire truck.

3 Write questions in the simple past.

1. how / he / a few hours / ago

   How was he a few hours ago?

2. it / start / a few minutes / ago

   _____

3. what / they / talk about

   _____

4. he / study / last night

   _____

5. they / at the library

   _____

6. why / you / think / that

   _____

7. we / sad / last year

   _____

4 Answer these questions with your own information.

1. How did you feel a few minutes ago?

   I was calm a few minutes ago.

2. Did you study English last night?

   _____

   _____

3. Where did you go last week?

   _____

   _____

4. Who did you text yesterday?

   _____

   _____

5. Did you see a movie last weekend?

   _____

   _____

1 Put the words in the correct order to make sentences to complete the conversation.

1. **A:** Who's / hero / your / ?
   Who's your hero?

2. **B:** think / I / are / athletes / heroes / .
   _____

3. **A:** mean / you / do / What / ?
   ⬭⬭⬭⬭⬭⬭⬭⬭⬭⬭⬭⬭⬭⬭⬭⬭⬭⬭

4. **B:** mean / athletes / I / hard / train / .
   _____

   at / are / the / They / their / best / sport / .
   _____

5. **A:** that / winners / heroes / Are / you / are / saying / ?
   _____
   _____

6. **B:** Not exactly. / make / that / What / to / say / heroes / is / us / try / I'm / harder / trying / .
   _____
   _____

2 Circle the phrases in Exercise 1 that ask for and give clarification.

3 Use the phrases to complete the conversations. There is more than one way to complete them.

> Are you saying that
> I mean
> ✓ What do you mean?
> What I'm trying to say is that

1. **A:** My heroes have always been cowboys.
   B: *What do you mean?*

2. **A:** I don't think business people are heroes.
   B: _____ they can't be heroes?

3. **A:** _____ superheroes are like real people.
   B: Oh, I see.

4. **A:** You think celebrities don't want to help others?
   B: _____ celebrities want to be *famous* for helping others.

1 Read about a hero. Then fill out the chart about her.

My hero is Serena Williams. She is famous because she is a great tennis player. In 2002, she became number one in the world for the first time. From 2002 to 2003, she held all four Grand Slam titles at the same time. She also won four Olympic medals.

I admire Serena Williams because she is a great tennis player. I also admire her because she is very strong and can come back to win after almost losing. Since she was brave enough to overcome her injuries, she can still play. She's also very kind and built a school in Kenya, Africa. Due to these reasons, she's my hero.

Who	Serena Williams
Her job	_____
Her personality	_____, _____, _____
Heroic things she has done	_____ _____ _____ _____
Why I admire her	_____ _____ _____ _____

2 Circle the connector words (*because, due to, since*) in Exercise 1. Then rewrite the sentences using different connector words.

1. _Since she is a great tennis player, she is famous._

2. _____
   _____

3. _____
   _____

4. _____
   _____

5. _____
   _____

3 Choose the correct connector words.

1. I admire Jane Goodall **since** / **due to** her work with chimpanzees.

2. Rick helps ocean animals **due to** / **because** he used to train them.

3. Erika has raced motorcycles **because** / **since** 2011.

4. **Due to** / **Since** his last movie, he's no longer popular.

5. **Since** / **Because** she works very hard, she is my role model.

4 Write sentences about your role model. Use connector words.

because	due to	since

1. _The Dalai Lama is my role model because_
   he is so calm.

2. _____
   _____

3. _____
   _____

4. _____
   _____

5. _____
   _____

1 Match the descriptions with the correct pictures. Then write the names of the places.

1. a place to buy shoes
_____

_____

a.

2. a place to get something to eat
_____

_____

b.

3. a place to deposit money _____

_____

c.

4. a place to get medicine _____

_____

d.

5. a place to buy many different things
_____

_____

e.

2 Look at the pictures. Circle the correct answers.

Jeff: Since I like to study wildlife, I want to be a ¹**lawyer / runner / scientist**. Because I'm ²**brave / funny / cheerful**, I can work with dangerous animals like snakes. And I'm ³**quiet / stubborn / serious**, so I can get close to them.

Nina: I love music. Ever since I was little, I've wanted to be a ⁴**singer / actor / painter**. I'm a good performer because I can be ⁵**kind / calm / stubborn** on stage. But I also need to be ⁶**quiet / serious / friendly** so I can talk to the audience between songs.

Alex: I love reading stories. Some people say I'm ⁷**cheerful / funny / kind** because I tell jokes. Other people say I'm ⁸**cheerful / serious / friendly** because I read a lot. I think I'd like to be a ⁹**soccer player / dancer / writer**. Then I could write funny stories.

3 Complete the sentences with the present continuous or simple present forms of the verbs.

1. I _____ (not watch) a movie right now.

2. She _____ (earn) money at her weekend job.

3. We usually _____ (spend) money on video games.

4. They _____ (deposit) the money into my account right now.

5. She _____ (lend) her cousins money every month.

4 Circle the correct answers.

1. **A:** How _____ money do you have?
   a. many   b. much   c. enough
   B: I have _____ money.
   a. any   b. enough   c. don't

2. **A:** Are there _____ shoes in your closet?
   a. many   b. how much   c. much
   B: Yes, _____.
   a. there is   b. there are   c. there aren't
   B: No, _____.
   a. there is   b. there isn't   c. there aren't

3. **A:** How _____ books do you have?
   a. much   b. any   c. many
   B: I don't have _____ books.
   a. many   b. much   c. some

4. **A:** _____ did you ride your bike last weekend?
   a. Where   b. When   c. Why
   B: I _____ to the beach.
   a. biking   b. am going   c. biked
                       to bike

5. **A:** Where is Tim _____ on his vacation?

    a. go   b. going to go c. went

    B: He _____ to the mountains.

    a. 's going   b. are going   c. goes
       to go

5 Circle the correct words. Then match the questions with the correct answers.

1. When **was / were / did** she go to China? _____

2. **Was / Were / Did** Lara play soccer last summer? _____

3. **Was / Were / Did** your friends visit last night? _____

4. Where **was / were / did** your cousins last weekend? _____

5. Where **was / were / did** Jason study last night? _____

a. No, she didn't.

b. They were at the pool.

c. She went in June.

d. He studied at the library.

e. Yes, they did.

6 Complete the sentences with the simple past.

Arline	Seth	Kyla
– study English on Wednesday	– play soccer Monday	– act in a movie in April
– go to Canada in June	– join soccer team in February	

1. Seth _____ soccer on Monday.

2. Arline _____ English on Wednesday.

3. Kyla _____ in a movie in April.

4. Arline _____ to Canada in June.

5. Seth _____ a soccer team in February.

7 Complete the conversations.

a lot of	lend
Are you saying that	much
borrow	started
enough	

Arthur: I really want to buy this hoodie!

Brittany: What do you like about it?

Arthur: It's made by a company that Bono [1]_____ in 2005. He's my hero.

Brittany: [2]_____ you'd buy that just because of Bono?

Arthur: Well, it looks cool, too.

Clerk: May I help you?

Arthur: I'd like to buy this hoodie.

Clerk: Here you are. That'll be $79.

Brittany: That's [3]_____ money!

Arthur: Oh no! I don't have [4]_____ money! Can I [5]_____ some?

Brittany: I don't have that [6]_____ money either. Maybe your hero Bono can [7]_____ it to you!

8 Answer the questions about your hero or role model. Write complete sentences.

1. Who is your hero or role model?

    _____

2. What is his or her job?

    _____

3. What heroic things does he or she do?

    _____

4. What is his or her personality like?

    _____

5. Why do you admire him or her?

    _____

6. When were you brave or heroic?

    _____

5 It's a Mystery!

Action verbs

1 Label the pictures with the words.

caught	fell	ran
chased	hid	stole
✓climbed	jumped	threw

1. _____climbed_____

2. _____

3. _____

4. _____

5. _____

6. _____

7. _____

8. _____

9. _____

2 Complete the story. Use the action verbs from Exercise 1.

The squirrel saw a nut up high in the tree. He ¹ __climbed__ the tree. The squirrel got the nut, but then a bird flew by, and the squirrel ² _____ out of the tree. But the squirrel still had the nut!

But the bird wanted the nut. The bird ³ _____ the squirrel. The squirrel ⁴ _____ behind the tree. He ⁵ _____ the nut under a leaf. Then the bird ⁶ _____ the nut.

As the bird flew away, the squirrel ⁷ _____ up on a log. He ⁸ _____ the bird by the leg.

But the bird ⁹ _____ the nut into the pond. The squirrel let go of the bird's leg. This time, no one got the nut!

3 Correct the sentences. Use the simple past.

    climbed
1. I ~~climb~~ trees a lot when I was young.
2. She said she never steal anything.
3. They hides the key under a rock.
4. She throw the ball really fast.
5. I catched the ball in my glove.
6. Did you see where she run?
7. The apple fells off the tree.
8. They jumpeds over the hole.
9. The dog chase his tail for an hour.

4 Write sentences using the action verbs from Exercise 1. Think of sports you play or activities you do. Use your own information.

1. *I climbed a tree last weekend.* _____
2. _____
3. _____
4. _____
5. _____

1 Match the questions with the answers.

1. What were you doing?
2. What was your friend Kevin doing?
3. What was the thief doing?
4. Was the police officer chasing her?
5. What was the thief wearing?
6. Was Kevin taking a picture with his phone?

a. He was using his phone.
b. Yes, he was.
c. No! He was texting and didn't see it.
d. I was buying a hat.
e. She was wearing a baseball cap.
f. She was stealing a hoodie.

2 Read the blog entry. Then answer the questions. Use the past continuous.

My Exciting Day
by Ken

Yesterday was an interesting day. I was skateboarding to school at 8:00 a.m. At about 8:05 a.m., I was passing the bank, and a man ran by me. He was carrying a bag, but he didn't look like he was exercising. He wasn't wearing running shoes. Next, a police officer ran up to me and asked if he could use my skateboard. I let him, of course. Then the police officer was skateboarding down the street! He was chasing the man with the bag. The police officer skated in front of the thief, and the thief fell. The police officer caught him!

1. What was Ken doing at 8:00 a.m.?

   He was skateboarding to school at 8:00 a.m.

2. What did Ken notice about the man's shoes?

   _____

3. What was the man carrying?

   _____

4. How was the police officer chasing the thief?

   _____

3 Unscramble the questions. Then answer the questions with information from the chart.

Last weekend	Last night	At 10:00 p.m.	This morning	At 9:00 a.m.
climbing a mountain	playing video games	sleeping	running a race	chasing a thief

1. night / doing / What / last / she / was / ?

   What was she doing last night?

   She was playing video games.

2. last / she / What / doing / weekend / was / ?

   _____

   _____

3. this / What / she / was / morning / doing / ?

   _____

   _____

4. she / homework / doing / 9:00 a.m. / at / Was / ?

   _____

   _____

5. 10:00 p.m. / at / doing / she / was / What / ?

   _____

   _____

4 Write questions in the past continuous. Answer the questions with your own information.

1. Where / you / live / last year?

   Where were you living last year?

   I was living in Brazil.

2. What / your friend / do / last weekend?

   _____

   _____

3. What / you / wear / yesterday afternoon?

   _____

   _____

4. What / you / do / this morning / at 8:00 a.m.?

   _____

   _____

5. What / you / watch / last night?

   _____

   _____

Adverbs of manner

1 Find eight more adverbs of manner.

✓badly	happily	loudly	quietly	terribly
carefully	hard	quickly	slowly	well

W	E	H	A	P	P	I	L	Y
E	Q	U	I	E	T	L	Y	A
L	H	A	R	D	W	E	L	L
L	T	E	R	R	I	B	L	Y
Q	U	I	C	K	L	Y	A	R
C	A	R	E	F	U	L	L	Y
E	L	O	U	D	L	Y	Y	I
E	E	A	S	L	O	W	L	Y
E	K	E	B	A	D	L	Y	R

2 Match each word with its opposite.

1. sadly   a. slowly

2. loudly   b. happily

3. well   c. badly

4. quickly   d. quietly

3 Complete the paragraph with the correct words.

| carefully | ✓ happily | hard | quickly | terribly |

I was [1] _____*happily*_____ playing my video game last night. It was a difficult game. I didn't want to make any mistakes, so I was playing [2] _____. I was trying really [3] _____, and maybe that's why I didn't hear the noise at first. But then it got louder. And then there was a bright light outside the window. I paused the game and went to the window. As I opened the curtain to look, an orange light [4] _____ flew by. And then it was gone. I don't know what it was! I was a little scared. After that, I went back to my game, and I played [5] _____.

4 Correct the incorrect sentences. Write *correct* if no changes are needed.

1. They did badly on the test. ___*correct*___

2. He played the piano ~~terrible~~. ___*terribly*___

3. The thief ran quickly. _____

4. I tried hardly to win the tennis match. _____

5. The turtle was walking slow. _____

6. We happily sang the birthday song. _____

7. The truck drove by loud. _____

8. We spoke quiet during the movie. _____

9. She was making the model careful. _____

5 Use adverbs of manner to answer the questions with your own information.

1. How do you read?

   I read slowly so I can enjoy the story.

2. How do you spend your money?

   _____

   _____

3. Do you walk slowly or quickly?

   _____

   _____

4. Do you play tennis well or badly?

   _____

   _____

Simple past vs. past continuous; *when* and *while*

1 Underline the past continuous.

While my sister and I <u>were watching</u> a movie, our dog came into the living room with us. When we were watching the exciting part, the dog started barking. My sister didn't notice the noise. But I did. So I put the dog out in the yard when my sister wasn't looking. Then I was getting snacks for us while my sister watched the movie. The phone was ringing while I was in the kitchen. I told my sister to answer it. She didn't, so I did. It was our neighbor. He saw our dog two blocks away! I gave my sister the snacks. Then I went out to look for the dog. She was watching another movie when I came home with the dog.

2 Match the phrases to make sentences.

1. I was playing soccer well

2. Helen saw the thief grab a hat

3. I heard the fire alarm

4. When we were hiking,

5. While it was raining,

a. while I was cooking dinner.

b. we stayed dry inside.

c. when I scored a goal.

d. we saw a deer with its baby.

e. while we were shopping.

3 Complete the sentences with *when* or *while*. Sometimes both answers are possible.

1. The picture fell loudly _____*when / while*_____ my brothers were playing.

2. I was using the computer _____ I heard the news.

3. _____ the team won, he was cheering loudly.

4. _____ she was surfing, she saw a shark.

5. I was hiking _____ I heard someone singing.

6. _____ he was playing the piano, we were listening happily.

4 Complete the conversation with the simple past or past continuous forms of the verbs.

Mark: Hey, I called you last night at 9:00.

Steve: I know. Sorry. I was watching the game when you ¹_____*called*_____ (call).

Mark: Yeah, well, while I ²_____ (watch) the game, our TV broke!

Steve: No! You missed the game! What ³_____ (happen) when it broke?

Mark: Spain was playing well when their center ⁴_____ (fall). The TV broke after that.

Steve: Well, you didn't miss much. After that, Spain was losing badly. I ⁵_____ (turn) the TV off when the game was almost over.

Mark: You didn't watch the ending! Do you know who won?

Steve: Yeah, I ⁶_____ (see) the headline when I was checking my email. Spain lost.

5 Use the verbs to write five sentences about events that were interrupted. Use your own information or write about someone you know.

| cooking | reading | ✓sleeping |
| playing | running | walking |

1. *I was sleeping when the storm began.*

2. _____

3. _____

4. _____

5. _____

Did I tell you about . . . ?

1 Complete the conversation. Put the words in the correct order to make sentences. More than one answer may be possible.

1. **Mei:** I / you / the / about / Did / movie / tell / ?

   Did I tell you about the movie? The one about a guy named Jeff who has these weird neighbors?

2. **Carlos:** No. / me / Tell / it / about / .

   _____

3. **Mei:** Jeff / the / was / sleeping / beginning, / In / .

   _____

4. Then / while / looked / talking / on / the /out of / the / was / window / Jeff / phone / he / .

   _____

   _____

5. his / watching / neighbors / was / He / .

   _____

6. **Carlos:** they / were / What / doing / ?

   _____

7. **Mei:** was / while / man / A / woman / in / her / bedroom / a letter / hid / reading / a / .

   _____

   _____

8. went / bedroom / there / man / the / the / and / was / screaming / into / Then / .

   _____

   _____

9. **Carlos:** weird / That's / .

   _____

10. happened / what / Then / ?

   _____

2 Choose the correct phrase to tell or react to a story.

Frank: [1]**That's weird / Did I tell you about** the play?

Olga: [2]**No, what happened? / Then what happened?**

Frank: Well, [3]**did I tell you / in the beginning**, the actor was saying his lines when the power went out.

Olga: [4]**In the beginning. / That's weird.**

Frank: Yeah, it was. Then there was a scream in the audience. We thought it was part of the play.

Olga: [5]**Then what happened? / Did I tell you?**

3 Complete the sentences.

✓Did I tell you about	In the beginning
That's weird	Then what happened

Sally: [1] _Did I tell you about_ my ski trip?

Jack: No. What happened?

Sally: [2] _____ I was skiing very carefully, and then I got tired. I started skiing badly.

Jack: Oh, oh. [3] _____?

Sally: Well, I jumped over a log and I landed badly. I fell into the deep snow. I heard a noise and thought my leg was broken. But my leg was fine.

Jack: [4] _____.

Sally: Yeah, it was strange. I really thought I broke my leg. But it was the sound of my ski breaking!

Jack: That's funny.

1 Put the parts of the story in order.

_____ But when I got there, the door was locked.
I didn't have a key. At first, I was surprised because I didn't lock the door. So who did?

_____ Then I heard barking. My dog was inside.
A few minutes later, he came to the door. Then he jumped on the door.

_1_ It was a dark and stormy night. I was feeding the animals in the barn when I heard the rain.
I closed the barn and ran to the house.

_____ In the end, I climbed in through a window.

_____ Then I thought maybe his foot locked the door on accident. After that, I was less scared. But I was wet from all the rain!

_____ Next, I was scared. What if someone was in the house?

2 Look at Exercise 1. Draw a square around the beginning and draw an X through the end. Then circle the sequencing words.

3 Rewrite the story above. Try to use only one sentence for each part.

At first	Later	✓One night
Finally	Next	Then

1. _One night, it started to rain._ _____

2. _____ I was surprised that _____.

3. _____ I was afraid that _____.

4. _____ my dog _____.

5. _____ I was less _____.

6. _____ I _____.

6 Home, Sweet Home

VOCABULARY Furniture and other household items

1 Put the letters in the correct order to make furniture and household words.

1. DEB _____bed_____

2. SEDK _____

3. OHREWS _____

4. LOTEIT _____

5. SEBAKOCO _____

6. REDSRES _____

7. FOAS _____

8. MARACHRI _____

9. RACIH _____

10. RORMRI _____

11. LETBA _____

12. BISTNACE _____

2 Label the pictures with the words from Exercise 1.

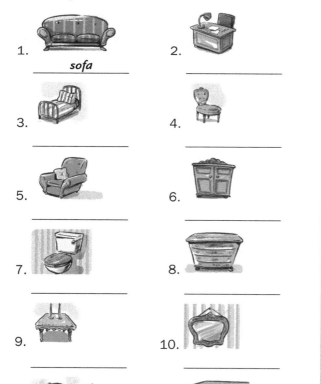

1. _____sofa_____

2. _____

3. _____

4. _____

5. _____

6. _____

7. _____

8. _____

9. _____

10. _____

11. _____

12. _____

3 Write the names of the furniture and household items from Exercise 1 in the correct columns.

Kitchen	Living room
chair	
Bathroom	**Bedroom**

4 Complete the sentences.

bed	cabinets	desk	mirror	✓sofa

1. I sit on a _____sofa_____ when I watch TV.

2. We keep cups and glasses in _____.

3. I sleep in a _____.

4. He does his homework at a _____.

5. Who do you see in the _____?

5 Answer the questions with your own information.

1. What's in your kitchen?

   _There's a table and chairs._____

2. What's your favorite thing to sit on?

   _____

3. What color is your bed?

   _____

4. What's in your dresser?

   _____

5. What's your favorite piece of furniture? Why?

   _____

   _____

GRAMMAR Comparative and superlative adjectives and adverbs

1 Complete the rules and write the comparative and superlative forms of the adjectives.

1. For most comparative adjectives and adverbs with one syllable, add _____*-er*_____.

    warm → ____*warmer*____

    long → _____

2. For most superlative adjectives and adverbs with one syllable, add _____.

    warm → the _____

    long → the _____

3. For most comparative adjectives and adverbs with two or more syllables, add _____.

    exciting → _____

    slowly → _____

4. For most superlatives adjectives and adverbs with two or more syllables, add _____.

    exciting → the _____

    slowly → the _____

5. Some comparative adjectives are irregular:

    good → _____

    bad → _____

6. Some superlative adjectives are irregular:

    good → the _____

    bad → the _____

7. Some comparative adverbs are irregular:

    well → _____

    badly → _____

8. Some superlative adverbs are irregular:

    well → the _____

    badly → the _____

2 Write the comparative and superlative forms of the adjectives.

Adjective	Comparative	Superlative
big	*bigger*	*the biggest*
strange		
beautiful		
exciting		

3 Write the comparative and superlative forms of the adverbs.

Adverb	Comparative	Superlative
quickly	*more quickly*	*the most quickly*
slowly		
far		
hard		

4 Complete the sentences using the comparative and superlative adjectives and adverbs.

1. My parents' living room is _____*nice*_____. But my grandparents' living room is _____*nicer*_____. (nice)

2. My brother's bedroom is the _____ bedroom in our house. It is _____ than our parents'. (big)

3. My sister cooks _____. But I cook _____. (well)

4. She speaks Spanish _____. But she speaks Chinese _____ Spanish. (quick)

5. In our house, the living room is _____ the dining room. But the kitchen is the _____. (popular)

6. Our bookcase is _____. But the dresser is _____. (dark)

VOCABULARY Household appliances

1 Complete the crossword puzzle with the names of household appliances.

Across clue row 1: `w a s h i n g m a c h i n e`

ACROSS

2.

3.

4.

5.

9.

10.

11.

12.

DOWN

1.

6.

7.

8.

2 Write the names of the household appliances.

1. This keeps your food cold. ___refrigerator___

2. You use these to cook food. _____,
_____, _____,
_____

3. You put your dishes in this to wash them.
_____

4. You clean your clothes in this. _____

5. You may need to use this on your shirt.
_____

6. This is probably the first thing you hear in the morning. _____

7. You might use this after your shower.
_____

8. When it's dark, you turn this on. _____

9. You clean the carpet with this. _____

3 What time of day do you use these appliances? Write the name of the appliance in the appropriate place in the word web. Add your own ideas. Some words can go in more than one circle.

| alarm clock | ✓dishwasher | hairdryer | lamp |
| microwave | refrigerator | stove | toaster |

Evening/Night
dishwasher
_____
_____

Day

Morning
_____
_____
_____

Afternoon
_____

_____

4 Write sentences about these household appliances. Use your own information.

| ✓alarm clock | dishwasher | hairdryer |
| iron | oven | vacuum cleaner |

1. I have a black ___alarm clock___ in my bedroom.

2. I rarely use the _____.

3. My favorite appliance is the _____.

4. I use the _____ in the _____.

5. _____.

GRAMMAR   should (not), (not) have to, must (not)

1 Circle the correct verbs to complete the rules in the chart.

should (not), (not) have to, must (not)
1. Use **should not** / **not have to** for advice and recommendations.
2. Use **must** / **have to** for responsibilities.
3. Use **not have to** / **must not** for things that are not required.
4. Use **must** / **have to** for an obligation.
5. Use **should not** / **must not** for a prohibition.

(In rule 1, "should not" is circled.)

2 Correct the sentences with the affirmative or negative.

shouldn't
1. You ~~should~~ keep bananas in the refrigerator.

2. You must not set your alarm clock if you want to wake up on time.

3. You don't have to follow the directions when you wash clothes.

4. You must look at your friend's test paper.

5. You don't have to keep your room clean to earn your allowance.

6. You have to do the dishes after dinner. Your brother is going to do them.

3 Write the correct answers.

1. (recommendation) You _____*should*_____ cook the vegetables on the stove and not in the microwave.

2. (prohibition) You _____ use the hairdryer while you're in the bathtub.

3. (responsibility) When his mother cooks, he _____ load the dishwasher after dinner.

4. (things not required) But he _____ do the dishes if he cooks dinner.

5. (obligation) Read the label. It says you _____ wash that shirt in cold water. Don't use hot water.

6. (things not required) We _____ bring a hairdryer. The hotel will have one.

4 Answer the questions. Use your own information and should (not), (not) have to, or must (not) to answer the questions.

1. What advice can you give someone about how to dress today?

   You should wear a T-shirt. It's hot outside.

2. What do you recommend NOT to do in school?

   _____
   _____

3. What do you have to do every night?

   _____
   _____

4. What don't you have to do on weekends?

   _____
   _____

5. What must you NOT eat?

   _____
   _____

1 Put the words in the correct order.

1. like / some / you / Would / help / ?

   Would you like some help?

2. Can / ask / you / a favor / I / ?

   _____

3. out / help / me / Could / you / ?

   _____

4. you / hand / a / give / I'll / .

   _____

2 Complete the conversation with the questions and statements from Exercise 1.

Tim: Are you going to the park?

Iris: Well, I want to, but you look too busy to come with me. ¹ *Would you like some help* ?

Tim: Yes, I would!

Iris: OK. What can I do?

Tim: I should move the sofa to clean behind it.
² _____ ?

Iris: Sure. ³ _____ .

Tim: Thanks. OK. And ⁴ _____
_____ ?

Iris: Of course. What is it?

Tim: Can you put those dishes in the dishwasher?

Iris: No problem.

3 Complete the conversations with the phrases from Exercise 1. More than one answer may be possible.

1. **A:** I need a hand in the garden.

   _____

   _____ ?

   B: Sorry, but I'm busy right now.

2. **A:** These boxes are heavy!

   B: _____

   _____ ?

   A: Thanks.

3. **A:** _____

   _____ ?

   I need a ride to school.

   B: I can drive you.

4. **A:** I need to vacuum and put the dishes in the dishwasher.

   B: _____

   _____ .

   A: Thank you!

READING TO WRITE

1 Write the words in the correct places in the chart.

apartment	chairs	modern
armchair	desk	new
bathroom	dishwasher	old
bed	dresser	small
bedroom	house	sofa
✓big	kitchen	table
bookcase	living room	washing machine

Size, age, kind	_____big_____, _____, _____, _____, _____, _____
Rooms	_____, _____, _____, _____
Furniture	_____, _____, _____, _____, _____, _____, _____, _____
Appliances	_____, _____

2 Correct the comma errors in the sentences. Some sentences may not need correction.

1. There are three armchairs, and one sofa in the living room.

2. I have to turn on the dishwasher brush my hair and set the alarm clock before bed.

3. We have a dog, a cat, and a bird.

4. He washes his bike and car every weekend.

5. Please put the cups glasses and dishes in the cabinets.

6. We cleaned the bathroom bedroom living room and kitchen this morning.

3 Answer the questions about you. Use the words from Exercise 1 and your own information.

1. What kind of home do you (or your friends) live in?

   I live in an apartment. But it's in London,

   so we call it a "flat."

2. What is your home like?

   _____

   _____

3. What is in your bedroom?

   _____

   _____

4. Where in your house do you spend the most time?

   _____

   _____

5. What is your favorite piece of furniture in your home?

   _____

   _____

1 Match the descriptions with the correct furniture and household items. Then write the names of the items.

1. This cooks food quickly. _____
   _____

   a.

2. This helps you see when a room is dark. _____
   _____

   b.

3. This is where you wash your whole body. _____
   _____

   c.

4. You keep clothing in this. _____
   _____

   d.

5. You put bread in this. _____
   _____

   e.

6. You can sit at this to eat a meal. _____
   _____

   f.

7. You use this in the bathroom every day. _____
   _____

   g.

8. This makes washing dishes easy. _____
   _____

   h.

9. You keep things to read here. _____
   _____

   i.

10. You get into this to sleep. _____
    _____

    j.

2 Complete the sentences with adverbs of manner.

1. She was talking _____ on her cell phone. (loud)

2. John usually does his homework _____. (careful)

3. Ella _____ cooked dinner for her parents. (happy)

4. They were singing _____ because they were nervous. (terrible)

5. She didn't practice, so the performance went _____. (bad)

6. I studied a lot, so I did _____ on my test. (good)

3 Complete the paragraph with action verbs.

| caught | chased | fell | jumped | stole |
| caught | climbed | hid | ran | threw |

The movie started as the thief [1]_____ in the bathroom at a bank. After everyone left in the evening, he [2]_____ a lot of money and put it into a bag. He left through the back door. Then he [3]_____ up the back of the next building. From there, he [4]_____ onto the next roof. You could hear sirens. The thief's buddy was waiting for him on the ground. The thief [5]_____ the bag down to his buddy. The buddy [6]_____ it and then [7]_____ away! The police saw him and [8]_____ him. The buddy [9]_____, and the police [10]_____ him! Meanwhile, the thief was holding another bag as he watched this from the roof!

4 Circle the correct answers.

1. I can bike _____ than I can run.

   a. more quickly   b. most quickly

2. He ran _____ today than ever before.

   a. farther   b. the farthest

3. She practiced a lot, and her playing got _____.

   a. better   b. the best

4. At night, it's _____ on the farm than it is in the city.

   a. darker   b. the darkest

5. I like movies more than TV, but I like books _____.

   a. better   b. the best

5 Complete the sentences with the correct forms of the verbs. Then write *past continuous* or *simple past*.

| jump | run | sing | talk |

1. I _____ while I was in the shower. _____

2. I _____ over the log when I fell. _____

3. _____ you _____ to Jillian on the phone last night when her sister sent you a text? _____

4. _____ Alan _____ in the race yesterday? _____

6 Complete the conversation.

Can I ask you for a favor?	not have to
Could you help me out?	should not
have to	Would you like some help?
I'll give you a hand.	
must not	

Manny: Want to go to the park now?

Claire: I'd love to! But I [1]_____ do all this laundry.

Manny: [2]_____

Claire: You [3]_____.

Manny: I know, but I want to.

Claire: Great! I need to put all this laundry in the washing machine. [4]_____

Manny: Sure. But wait a minute! You [5]_____ wash light and dark colors together. You must look at the labels first!

Claire: Oh! I never do that.

Manny: [6]_____ I'll separate the colors into light and dark.

Claire: Great. You do that. I'll get the laundry soap. Oops. [7]_____

Manny: Sure, what is it?

Claire: Can you reach the soap?

Manny: OK. Next time you [8]_____ put it up so high.

Claire: I didn't put it up there. I never do the laundry!

7 Visions of the Future

VOCABULARY Computers and communication

1 Find eight more computer words.

O	V	G	K	E	Y	B	O	A	R	D	F
L	Q	T	E	H	K	F	Y	P	A	O	L
T	O	U	C	H	S	C	R	E	E	N	A
L	P	T	O	U	C	H	P	A	D	E	S
Q	X	F	L	A	S	H	D	R	I	V	E
E	H	C	Y	F	T	A	B	L	E	T	D
I	M	I	T	Z	G	C	J	N	Q	Y	R
S	M	A	R	T	P	H	O	N	E	S	I
E	D	I	R	D	H	R	A	L	F	L	V
M	P	R	I	N	T	E	R	C	W	X	E
B	P	V	S	O	P	N	W	I	F	I	A
L	G	M	O	U	S	E	J	P	P	I	F

2 Complete the sentences. Use the computer words from Exercise 1.

1. You don't need a mouse for your laptop because you can use the ___touch pad___ .

2. Save your work on a _____ so you can use it with another computer.

3. The _____ wasn't working, so we couldn't get on the Internet.

4. My mom prefers typing on the _____ to using the touch pad.

5. I prefer using a _____ to using a laptop.

6. I don't use my _____ very often. I email most of my assignments to my teacher.

3 Use the phrases and the computer words from Exercise 1 to write sentences.

communicate with friends	do homework
✓computing power	save information

1. *A smartphone today has more computing power than the first computers.*

2. _____

   _____

3. _____

   _____

4. _____

   _____

4 Complete the sentences with your own information. Use the computer words from Exercise 1.

1. I have a _____*tablet and a smartphone*_____ .

2. I use a _____ to _____ .

3. I never use a _____ .

4. My parents _____ .

5. My best friend _____ .

GRAMMAR *will* and *won't* for predictions

1 **Rewrite the underlined phrases as contractions.**

They'll
1. <u>Computers will</u> be smarter in the future.

2. <u>This tablet will</u> get smaller in the future.

3. <u>My family will not</u> use a mouse in the future.

4. <u>You will not</u> cook your own meals.

5. <u>He will</u> use his smartphone to buy everything.

GRAMMAR Adverbs of possibility

2 **Complete the chart using the adverbs of possibility.**

certainly	maybe	probably
✓definitely	perhaps	

Sure	*definitely* _____
Pretty sure	_____
Not as sure	_____ _____

3 **Put the words in the correct order to make sentences.**

1. will / planes / fly / Robots / probably / .

   Robots will probably fly planes.

2. future / we / use / Perhaps / in / won't / the / paper / .

   _____

   _____

3. our / Robots / houses / certainly / will / clean / .

   _____

   _____

4. have / our / clothes / them / will / touch screens / Maybe / in / .

   _____

   _____

5. company / I'll / for / software / work / a / definitely / .

   _____

   _____

4 **Answer the questions using *will* and *won't* to predict the future. Use adverbs of possibility.**

1. What will cars do in the future?

   They'll definitely drive themselves.

2. How will we use robots in the future?

   _____

   _____

3. Will bikes fly in the future?

   _____

   _____

4. Will we have cameras in our jewelry in the future?

   _____

   _____

5. How will you be different in the future?

   _____

   _____

VOCABULARY Technology verbs

1 Complete the technology verbs.

down	down	down	in	in
✓on	on	out	up	up

1. turn ___on___
2. zoom _____
3. click _____
4. zoom _____
5. back _____
6. sign _____
7. scroll _____
8. sign _____
9. scroll _____
10. shut _____

2 Write the technology verbs from Exercise 1. Some will be pairs of verbs.

1. ___scroll up___
   ___scroll down___

2. _____
   _____

3. _____

4. _____
   _____

5. _____

6. _____

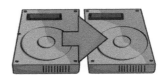

7. _____

3 Circle the correct technology verbs.

1. Can you (zoom in) / sign out so we can see it better?

2. Did you **turn on** / **back up** your homework on the flash drive?

3. Don't forget the password or you won't be able to **sign in** / **zoom out**.

4. **Back up** / **Click on** this link to read the blog.

5. **Shut down** / **Scroll up** to look at the picture again.

4 Write sentences. Use technology verbs and your own information.

1. my email

   I never sign out of my email.

2. my school's website

   _____
   _____

3. my computer

   _____
   _____

4. my picture

   _____
   _____

5. my favorite website

   _____
   _____

First conditional with
will (*not*), *may* (*not*), and *might* (*not*)

1 Circle the correct words.

1. If her laptop **breaks** / **might break**, her parents **buys** / **might buy** her a new one.

2. You **won't win** / **won't** the game if you **choose** / **won't choose** that character.

3. If you **get** / **will get** some money, what **you buy** / **will you buy**?

4. You **see** / **will see** it better if you **zoom in** / **might zoom in**.

5. **Will study** / **Will she study** science when she **goes** / **may goes** to college?

6. They **not get** / **may not get** good grades if they **study** / **don't study** harder.

2 Put the words in the correct order to make sentences.

1. of / yours / kind / will / stops / working / you / if / What / phone / get / ?

   What kind of phone will you get if yours

   stops working?

2. not / don't / get / a / money / tablet / I / I may / save / if / .

   _____

   _____

3. the fastest / you / play / new / a / computer / want to / video games, / you / might / need / If / .

   _____

   _____

4. back up / may / lose / them / If / our / photos, / we / we / don't / .

   _____

   _____

5. video game / make / learns to / kind of / will / he / if he / code / What / write / ?

   _____

   _____

3 Correct the sentences.

1. If you click on this link you see the video.
   (*, will* inserted)

2. Will you sign into my account if I may give you my password?

3. He may not see the text message if his phone might be off.

4. We not have Wi-Fi if we sit in the library.

5. If you will play the game, first you may not like the movie.

6. How you buy a tablet if you don't save your money?

4 Change the affirmative sentences to negative sentences and the negative sentences to affirmative sentences.

1. You'll answer your smartphone if you go to the movies. (*won't*)

2. If there are girl characters, I won't play that video game.

3. We'll back up our files if we get a flash drive.

4. If Helen decides to watch a video, she'll choose a comedy.

5. If I post videos, they won't be cat videos.

5 Complete the questions and sentences with *will* (*not*), *may* (*not*), or *might* (*not*) and your own ideas.

1. If I don't do well in computer class,
   I might not get a computer job.

2. What kind of video will you post _____
   _____?

3. If I have a blog in the future, _____
   _____.

4. Will you buy a _____ if you _____
   _____?

CONVERSATION Using your cell phone

1 Put the words in order to make questions and answers.

1. do / upload / I / How / a / photo / ?

   How do I upload a photo?

2. need / You / click / to / picture / the / icon / on / .

   _____

3. How / does / touch pad / work / this / ?

   _____

4. you / to / All / do / have / touch / the / is / screen / .

   _____

   _____

2 Complete the sentences.

All you have to	✔ How does it work?
how do I	you need to

Grandmother: Let's take a photo with your smartphone. ¹ *How does it work?*

Boy: First, ² _____ press the round button to turn it on.

Grandmother: Oh, look! There we are. Now, ³ _____ take the picture?

Boy: ⁴ _____ do is press this big button.

Grandmother: And there's our picture. That was easy!

3 Write the questions or answers. Use the phrases and your own ideas.

All you have to	✔ How do I	How do I
How does _____	work?	You need to

1. Ask someone for instructions to send a text.

   How do I send a text?

2. Ask someone how to use a GPS watch.

   _____

   _____

3. Tell someone how to turn on a digital camera.

   _____

   _____

4. Tell someone how to listen to music.

   _____

   _____

5. Ask someone how to watch a video.

   _____

   _____

1 Read the opinion paragraph. Then label the parts: underline the introduction and conclusion. Put a box around the reasons. Circle any facts or examples.

Future Robot Doctors
by Bill Lee

<u>I believe that in the future, when you go to see a doctor, you will see a robot, not a human doctor.</u> One reason I think that is because more and more doctors are using computers to help their patients. The last time I went to a doctor, she used her smartphone to look up what medicine to give me. Another reason I think we will see robots for a cough or cold is that they will give human doctors more time to spend with really sick people. This will save time and money. And another reason is that unlike human doctors, robots don't get sick! If you sneeze on the robot, it won't catch your cold. This way, doctors won't get sick. In conclusion, I think in the future, we will see robot doctors for colds and simple illnesses.

2 Complete the sentences with the opinion and reason phrases. Then number the sentences in order. More than one answer may be possible.

> Another reason is (that)
> For these reasons,
> I think (that)
> In conclusion
> ✓ In my opinion,
> One reason is (that)

_____ _____ people will be able to help each other directly.

_____ _____ people won't need to use money.

_____ _____ we are already doing this, for example with computer code that people share.

_____ _____ we won't need to use money because we will trade everything.

_____ _____ people can easily connect with other people over the Internet. This lets them trade services with each other.

_1_ _In my opinion,_ I believe that in the future, we won't use money.

3 Complete number 1 with an opinion. Complete numbers 2–4 with reasons for that opinion. Complete number 5 with a conclusion. Use your own ideas.

1. In my opinion, _____
_____
_____

2. I think (that) _____
_____
_____.

3. One reason is (that) _____
_____
_____.

4. Another reason is (that) _____
_____
_____.

5. For these reasons, _____
_____
_____.

The Choices We Make

VOCABULARY Life events

1 Put the letters in the correct order to make life events.

1. OG OT LEGLOCE

_____

2. TEAK A REYA FOF

_____

NEW YORK STATE

DRIVER'S LICENSE

3. GTE ROUY VIRRED'S SINELCE

_____

4. REETIR

_____*retire*_____

5. OG OT CLOSOH

_____

6. EB NOBR

_____

7. TEG A OJB

_____

8. NIFHIS OLOHCS

_____

9. EHVA DHINCELR

_____

10. ETG ERIDMRA

_____

2 What are these things? Write the life events from Exercise 1.

1. Before you buy a car, you need to pass a test to do this.

   _____*get your driver's license*_____

2. This is something you do after you've worked for a very long time.

   _____

3. People do this when they are in love and want to be together forever.

   _____

4. You will have teachers when you do this.

   _____

   And you will have professors when you do this.

   _____

5. You will make money when you do this.

   _____

6. This is the first thing you ever do.

   _____

3 Complete the sentences. Use forms of the words from Exercise 1.

1. Julian's grandfather _____*retired*_____ from his job. He worked at the school for 30 years.

2. Tim's little brother is excited because he's finally old enough to _____.

3. First, you _____, and every year after that, you celebrate your birthday.

4. If my mom _____ at the mall, she'll need to _____ and buy a car because it's too far to walk.

5. After she _____ in June, she wants to _____ and travel before she _____.

1 Choose the correct words.

1. Use **be going to** / **will** to talk about plans in the future.

2. Use **be going to** / **will** to talk about predictions and unplanned decisions.

3. What is he **to do** / **going to do**?

   He is going **to play** / **play** basketball.

   He isn't going **do** / **to do** his homework.

4. Where will she travel first?

   She'll travel / **She travel** to China first.

   She not travel / **She won't travel** to China first.

5. Is he going **study** / **to study** biology?

   Yes, he is. / **Yes, he study.**

   No, he's not going. / **No, he isn't.**

6. **Going to** / **Will** they get married?

   Yes, they **will** / **going to**.

   No, they **aren't going to** / **won't**.

2 Complete the conversation with *be going to* or *will*.

Jody: Hi, Scott. Congratulations on finishing school!

Scott: Thanks! You, too. What ¹_____ *are* _____ you ___ *going to* ___ do now?

Jody: I ²_____ go to college in the fall. I got into the Art Academy.

Scott: ³_____ you _____ study art?

Jody: Not exactly. I ⁴_____ study animation.

Scott: That's great.

Jody: What about you? What ⁵_____ you _____ do?

Scott: I'm not sure yet. Maybe I ⁶_____ take a year off and travel.

Jody: That sounds exciting.

Scott: Yeah, but my dad wants me to get a job at his company. I ⁷_____ probably travel in the summer and work in the fall.

3 Unscramble the sentences and questions.

1. probably / you / won't / He / listen / to / .

   He probably won't listen to you.

2. won't / thinks / after-school / get / she / job / She / an / .

   _____

   _____

3. year / off / they'll / take / Maybe / a / .

   _____

4. Australia / will / to / When / travel / Jack / ?

   _____

4 Complete the questions with *be going to* or *will*. Then answer the questions with your own information.

1. When _____ *will* _____ you finish school?

   _____

2. When _____ you get your driver's license?

   _____

3. Where _____ you live in 10 years?

   _____

4. Is your friend _____ go to college with you?

   _____

5. Are you _____ get married soon?

   _____

Containers and materials

1 **What materials are they made of? Write the container words in the chart.**

1. Plastic

   bottle

   _____

2. Paper and cardboard

   _____

   _____

3. Glass

   _____

   _____

4. Cloth

   _____

5. Metal

   _____

2 **Circle the correct words.**

1. We bring our groceries home in a (cloth bag)/ **metal can**.

2. At the supermarket, we put the apples in a **glass jar / paper bag**.

3. Shampoo comes in a **plastic bottle / cardboard box**.

4. My mother bought a **plastic carton / cloth bag** of orange juice.

5. I recycled the **glass jar / cardboard box** that my new shoes came in.

6. If you wash the **glass jar / metal can** the peanut butter came in, you can use it again.

7. I prefer to drink soda from a **cloth bag / glass bottle**, not a **cloth bag / metal can**.

3 **Use container words and your own information to write sentences.**

1. (recycle / cardboard box)
   We recycle cardboard boxes at my house.

2. (reuse / cloth bag)

   _____

   _____

3. (not / paper bag)

   _____

   _____

4. (metal can)

   _____

   _____

5. (plastic carton)

   _____

   _____

GRAMMAR Present continuous and simple present for future

1 Put the words in the correct order to ask questions. Use contractions if possible. Then match the questions with the answers.

1. helping / the / they / dolphins / Are / ?

   <u>Are they helping the</u>
   <u>dolphins?</u>   <u>b</u>

2. hour / the / Does / leave / bus / in / an / ?

   _____

   _____ _____

3. Ben / is / Why / making / video / a / ?

   _____

   _____ _____

4. they / have / the / When / meeting / do / ?

   _____

   _____ _____

5. plastic / are / collecting / How / they / the / ?

   _____

   _____ _____

6. to / do / go / you / When / Japan / ?

   _____

   _____ _____

a. They're using a bucket.

b. Yes, they are.

c. I go next month.

d. No, it doesn't.

e. He's teaching people about dolphins.

f. They have the meeting next Saturday.

2 Complete the sentences with the present continuous or simple present.

1. I <u>'m buying</u> shoes made from recycled plastic bottles. (buy)

2. The plastic bag recycling drive _____ on June 3. (end)

3. Our town _____ a recycling program. (start)

4. At what time on Tuesday _____ he _____ for Costa Rica? (leave)

5. They _____ to school. (not drive)

3 Use the information in the invitation to complete the questions and answers with the present continuous or simple present.

Who?	You are invited to Kim's birthday party!
What?	Celebrate Kim's birthday. No need to buy gifts. We'll make them!
How?	Collect plastic bags, paper bags, and cardboard from your home and bring them to the party. We'll learn how to recycle them into fun gifts.
Where?	The Art of Recycling Center
When?	Saturday, October 12, at noon Be green! Ride your bike or take the bus.

1. <u>Does</u> the party <u>start</u> at noon? (start)

   <u>Yes, it does.</u> _____

2. Where _____ you _____ on Saturday? (go)

   _____

3. _____ you _____ gifts? (buy)

   _____

4. What _____ you _____ from home? (bring)

   _____

5. What _____ you _____ at The Art of Recycling Center? (learn to do)

   _____

4 Answer the questions with the simple present or present continuous and your own information.

1. Are you going to recycle anything next week?

   <u>Yes, I am.</u> _____

2. When does your family recycle things?

   _____

3. What things are you going to reuse?

   _____

4. What does your family *not* recycle?

   _____

1 Complete the conversation.

> Absolutely!   ✓ I think
> I disagree.   Maybe, but I think
> I suppose you're right.

Ingrid: Well, that was an interesting assignment!

Ted: A paper about "What I plan to do after I finish school"? That's easy!

Ingrid: You think so? What *are* you going to do after you finish school?

Ted: I want to study marine biology and the environment. Then I'm going to get a job that helps the ocean. ¹_____*I think*_____ it's the most important part of the planet.

Ingrid: ²_____ people are the most important part of the planet.

Ted: People? ³_____ People cause the pollution!

Ingrid: ⁴_____ That's why the most important thing we can do is change how people do things.

Ted: Hmm. I hadn't thought of it that way. ⁵_____ So what are you going to after you finish school?

Ingrid: I'm going to study environmental law!

Ted: Cool! Maybe we can work together.

2 Write a response that agrees or disagrees with each statement. Use the words in the box and your own ideas.

> Absolutely!
> I disagree.
> I suppose you're right.
> Maybe, but I think

1. Everyone should study a foreign language.

   _____

   _____

2. I don't think people should eat meat.

   _____

   _____

3. I think everyone should get married.

   _____

   _____

4. I think everyone should have 10 children.

   _____

   _____

5. I think it might be fun to be the leader of a country.

   _____

   _____

To: Ashley Morrison
From: Ben Smith
Subject: Summer Volunteer Opportunity

Dear Ms. Morrison,

I am interested in volunteering at the Senior Center this summer.

I'd like to be a scientist and work with animals someday. I train dogs to be "service dogs." Service dogs help people who can't see or hear well. I train the dogs to visit with people. I think service dogs help people to feel better.

I want to help older people. My grandfather is sick, and I help him. I bring my service dog when I visit my grandfather. It really cheers him up. He is doing much better now.

I have a very well-trained dog named Max, and I'd like to bring him to the Senior Center to visit the older people. I'd volunteer by myself, but I'd rather bring Max with me. Thank you for considering us for the volunteer position.

Sincerely,

Ben (and Max the dog)

1 Read Ben's email. Complete the word web.

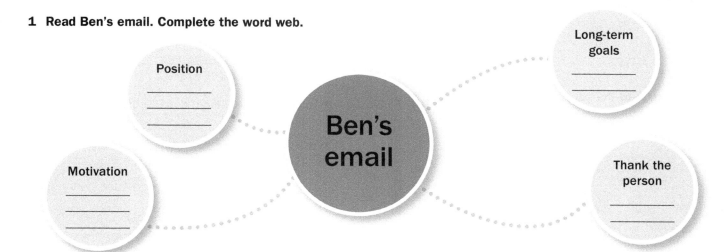

Long-term goals
_____
_____

Position
_____
_____
_____

Ben's email

Motivation
_____
_____
_____

Thank the person
_____
_____

2 Circle examples of *want*, *would like* (*to*), and *would rather* (*'d rather*) in Ben's email.

3 Complete the sentences using *want*, *would like* (*to*), and *would rather* (*'d rather*). Use contractions. More than one answer may be possible.

1. She wants to be a doctor. She _'d like to_____ work with children.

2. He _____ volunteer at the recycling center. He'd like to help people learn about recycling.

3. Ken wants to work outdoors. He _____ work in a park than an office.

4. Jillian and Bob _____ help people to lose weight.

5. Paula _____ help sea turtles. She _____ start a volunteer program at the beach than join one online.

1 Label each object. Then underline the materials words, circle the container words, and draw a box around the computer words.

a cardboard box	a metal can
a cloth bag	a paper bag
a glass bottle	a plastic carton
a keyboard	a touch pad
a flash drive	Wi-Fi

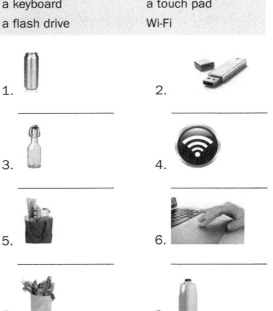

1. _____
2. _____

3. _____
4. _____

5. _____
6. _____

7. _____
8. _____

9. _____
10. _____

2 Complete the conversation with the words in the box.

Click on	sign in
finished school	smartphone
going to college	tablet
How do I	take a year off
printer	You need to

Hannah: My sister just ¹_____. We had a big party. Want to see some photos? I have them on my ²_____.

Stella: Sure. But let's use my ³_____. The screen is bigger.

Hannah: Good idea. Where do I ⁴_____ to the website?

Stella: ⁵_____ this button.

Hannah: OK. Here they are.

Stella: Nice. She got a lot of gifts! Why is she holding that T-shirt?

Hannah: It's where she's ⁶_____ next year.

Stella: Isn't she going this fall?

Hannah: No, she isn't. She's going to ⁷_____. She wants to volunteer in the rainforest in Costa Rica.

Stella: Wow. That's far away.

Hannah: I can show you where she will be on this map. ⁸_____ zoom in?

Stella: ⁹_____ move your fingers like this.

Hannah: Thanks. Here's the website.

3 Write sentences in the future tense with *will* or *won't*.

1. We don't need a keyboard or mouse. (probably)

_____

2. Computers think like humans. (perhaps)

_____

3. Clothing and jewelry have touchscreen technology in them. (maybe)

_____

4. My sister doesn't turn in printed papers for school. (definitely)

_____

5. I don't go anywhere without my smartphone. (certainly)

_____

4 Match the phrases to make sentences and questions.

1. If I make a video in the future, _____
2. What will he do _____
3. My friends may not be happy _____
4. If you buy a new smartphone, _____
5. He won't lose his files _____

a. if he backs them up regularly.
b. if I write about them on my blog.
c. which one will you buy?
d. if his smartphone breaks?
e. it won't be a cat video.

5 Answer the questions about Danielle's email (on the right) using *be going to* and *will*.

1. What's Danielle going to do after finishing school?

_____
_____

2. Who might she live with?

_____
_____

3. Where will she go first?

_____
_____

4. How will she get money to travel?

_____
_____

5. What is she going to study in college?

_____
_____

To carla_g
From danigarcia
Subject I miss you!

Dear Aunt Carla,

How are things in Argentina? I miss you! I'm going to take a year off when I finish school. I'm not going to start college right away. I think it's important to travel and see the world. Mom disagrees with me, though. She wants me to start college right away. But I'd rather travel and learn languages and meet new people. If I save money from my after-school job, I might be able to travel for a year.

If your invitation is still open, would you like a visitor? I'd like to visit you in Argentina to start my year off. I won't stay too long. Mom said that maybe I can help in your restaurant. I'd really like that because I want to study hospitality. What do you think of my plan?

Love,

Daniela

6 Agree or disagree with the following statements. Use your own ideas. Give reasons for your opinions.

| Absolutely! | I disagree. | I suppose you're right. |

1. In the future, you'll probably have a flying car.

_____
_____

2. In the future, you'll definitely be rich and famous.

_____
_____

3. In the future, you're probably going to live in your hometown.

_____
_____

4. In the future, you're going to retire at age 30.

_____
_____

9 Watch Out!

VOCABULARY Accident and injury verbs

1 Find nine more words for accidents and injuries.

✓ bang	burn	cut	hurt	sprain
break	crash	fall off	slip	trip

O	Q	F	A	L	L	O	F	F
J	Y	Z	B	A	N	G	D	N
U	H	U	R	T	T	R	I	P
I	U	S	L	I	P	P	Y	M
S	P	R	A	I	N	S	E	Q
K	G	P	W	W	J	N	Y	M
H	Y	J	E	B	U	R	N	H
V	C	U	T	B	R	E	A	K
Q	G	Y	Z	C	R	A	S	H

2 Label the pictures with the words from Exercise 1.

1. _____ *fall off* _____

2. _____

3. _____

4. _____

5. _____

6. _____

7. _____

8. _____

9. _____

10. _____

3 Complete the article with the accidents and injuries words from Exercise 1.

It's difficult being a teen. Teens often [1] _____ *crash* _____ their bikes and get injured playing sports. But did you know that injuries happen to people over age 65, too? The number one injury might surprise you:

Falling down

Older people often [2] _____ down in the kitchen or on the stairs. They might [3] _____ on the stairs or [4] _____ on a wet kitchen floor. Twisting an ankle when falling down is one way people can [5] _____ an ankle. Falling down can [6] _____ the back and cause back pain. For older people, falling down can be very serious. Their bones can [7] _____ easily, especially their hips.

A fall can create other injuries, too. A person might [8] _____ his or her head on something, or even [9] _____ it on something sharp. Older people can avoid falling by wearing good shoes and keeping the floor clear of items they can trip over.

GRAMMAR Present perfect statements with regular and irregular verbs

1 Write the past participle of the verbs. Then underline the verbs that are irregular.

Verb	Past participle
1. burn	*burned*
2. live	
3. slip	
4. study	
5. do	
6. fly	
7. lose	
8. take	

2 Complete the chart. Use *has/have* and the past participle of the words to form the present perfect. More than one answer may be possible.

been	burned	hurt	✓ sprained
broken	happened	seen	tripped

	Affirmative
Regular	Ken ¹ ___*has sprained*___ his finger playing basketball many times.
	More falling accidents ² _____ to older people.
	Negative
	Tessa ³_____ on the stairs before.
	We ⁴_____ never _____ any food in the oven before.

Irregular	Affirmative
	Ella ⁵_____ to Bogota twice.
	More older people ⁶_____ a hip than younger people.
	Negative
	Mark ⁷_____ his back before.
	We ⁸_____ our team win before.

3 Write the present perfect affirmative (✓) and negative (✗) statements using the verbs from Exercise 1.

1. I ___*haven't burned*___ my fingers on a hot stove in months. (✗)

2. My team _____ more games than we have won. (✓)

3. Elizabeth _____ for the test. (✓)

4. We _____ dangerous things like this before. (✗)

5. Jack _____ in a helicopter before. (✗)

6. I _____ in this town for a long time. (✓)

7. They _____ the same bus to school for years. (✓)

8. Pete _____ on the ice during a hockey game before. (✗)

4 Use these phrases to write affirmative and negative present perfect sentences with your own information.

1. broke my arm

I've never broken my arm before.

2. fly to Alaska

_____

3. fall off a bike

_____

4. sprain an ankle

_____

5. sing on stage

_____

VOCABULARY Parts of the body

1 Unscramble the words.

1. OFOT _____foot_____

2. EKEN _____

3. STEO _____

4. RSWIT _____

5. DRSLOHUE _____

6. KELNA _____

7. COHMAST _____

8. KECN _____

9. BOLEW _____

2 Label the pictures with the words from Exercise 1.

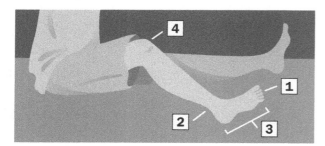

1. _____toes_____   2. _____
3. _____   4. _____

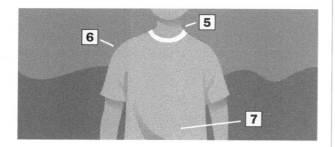

5. _____   6. _____
7. _____

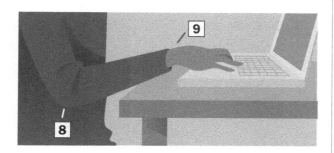

8. _____   9. _____

3 Complete the sentences with the words from Exercise 1.

1. This is at the top of your arm. _____shoulder_____

2. Your head sits on top of this. _____

3. You wear shoes on these. _____

4. You use this to move your foot. _____

5. You can wear a watch or a bracelet on this.

   _____

6. This is where food goes.

7. This is where the leg bends. _____

8. This is where the arm bends. _____

9. You have 10 of these on your foot.

   _____

4 Complete the conversation.

ankle	knee	wrist
✓ elbow	shoulder	

Phillip: Hi, Rita! Hey, what happened to your wrist?

Rita: I was playing volleyball with Olivia last weekend. The ball came over the net, so I jumped up to hit it. But Olivia jumped up at the same time. I bent my arm, and my [1] _____elbow_____ hit her on the [2] _____. I'm glad I didn't hit her head. But she fell and twisted her [3] _____ when she landed.

Phillip: Ouch!

Rita: Well, it gets worse. Olivia couldn't stand up at all! I went over to help her, but I slipped and fell. And I bent my [4] _____ too far when I landed on my hand. I think it's sprained. We're going to miss several volleyball games.

Phillip: I know how you feel. I was running during soccer practice and fell. I landed on my [5] _____. It really hurts to bend my leg now.

Rita: I guess we'll just have to *watch* our games for now!

GRAMMAR Present perfect questions; present perfect vs. simple past

1 Match the questions with the correct answers.

1. Why has he had so many accidents?
2. Has she ever fallen down the stairs?
3. What happened on your vacation?
4. What bones have you broken?
5. Have you ever banged your head?
6. Have you ever sprained your ankle?

a. No, she hasn't.
b. Yes, I have.
c. Because he's clumsy.
d. I tripped and fell. I hurt my wrist.
e. Yes, I have. I sprained it yesterday.
f. My arm and my finger.

2 Complete the questions in the present perfect.

1. **A:** ___Have___ you ___ever gone___ windsurfing? (ever, go)

   B: No, we haven't.

2. **A:** _____ you _____ in a helicopter? (ever, ride)

   B: Yes, I have. I rode in one last week.

3. **A:** _____ they _____ Portuguese? (ever, study)

   B: Yes, they have.

4. **A:** Where _____ you _____? (live)

   B: In Guadalajara and New York.

5. **A:** Why _____ he _____ the bus every day this week? (take)

   B: Because his bike is broken.

6. **A:** _____ she _____ a video? (ever, make)

   B: No, she hasn't.

3 Use the chart to write the questions and answers.

Who?	Doing what?	How?	What injury?	When?
Kate	dancing	trip	sprain ankle	in the past
George	biking	fall	none	never
Stacey	hockey	slip	broken wrist	last winter
Brian	car accident	crash	hurt neck	last May
Maria	surfing	fall off	hurt shoulder	on vacation

1. ___Has___ Kate ___ever sprained___ her ankle?

   Yes, she ___has___.

2. _____ George _____ off his bike?

   No, he _____.

3. Stacey, _____ you _____ playing hockey?

   Yes, I _____.

   When?

   _____.

4. Brian, what _____ last May?

   _____

5. Maria, _____ you _____ off your surfboard?

   _____

   What _____?

   _____

4 Answer the questions with your own information. Write complete sentences.

1. Have you ever lost your backpack?

   Yes, I have. I lost it last week.

2. Have you ever broken any bones?

   _____

   _____

3. Have you ever tried to surf?

   _____

   _____

4. Have you ever traveled to another country?

   _____

   _____

5. What good books have you read?

   _____

   _____

CONVERSATION Good news, bad news

1 Complete the conversation with the words to react to good news and bad news.

> ✓ I'm sorry to hear that.   That's cool!
>
> That sounds like fun.   that's too bad

Emily: Hi, Zack. How was your camping trip?

Zack: It was good and bad, I guess. First, the bad news – Jim climbed a tree, fell out of the tree, and landed in the fire!

Emily: Oh no! ¹ *I'm sorry to hear that.* Is he OK?

Zack: He's fine, but he burned part of his shoe.

Emily: Oh, ²_____ about the shoe.

Zack: I know. But it gets better . . . I took a video of him falling out of the tree and put it on my website. It's gotten more than 10,000 views so far.

Emily: ³_____

Zack: Yeah! It is! And the local news heard about it. So we are going to be on TV.

Emily: Wow! ⁴_____

2 Correct the reactions. Mark (✓) if the reaction is correct. Use the expressions from Exercise 1.

1. **A:** I'm going to Hawaii for vacation!

   B: ~~I'm sorry to hear that.~~

   That sounds like fun. _____

2. **A:** I'm sorry I can't come to your party on Saturday.

   B: That's cool.

   _____

3. **A:** My bike was stolen yesterday.

   B: That's too bad.

   _____

4. **A:** I made a new friend in guitar class.

   B: I'm sorry to hear that.

   _____

5. **A:** She broke her arm skateboarding.

   B: That's cool.

   _____

3 Write a reaction to each sentence. Use the phrases from Exercise 1.

1. **A:** My pet turtle died.

   B: _____

2. **A:** I won the skateboard competition!

   B: _____

3. **A:** We are going to the swimming pool this weekend.

   B: _____

4. **A:** I can't go to the movie tonight because I have to do homework.

   B: _____

READING TO WRITE

1 Number the paragraphs to put the parts of the email in the correct order.

To Adriana S.
From Laurel M.
Subject Party invitation

Hi Adriana,

_____ We're going to take her to Donner Lake. She used to sail there when she was a girl. So, my Dad rented a sailboat to take her out. She doesn't know about it yet. It's a surprise!

_____ Again, I'm really sorry. Have a great time! Text me some pictures. Maybe we can go to a concert together next month.

_____ I'd love to come, but I can't go with you.

__1__ Thanks for inviting me to the concert on Saturday.

_____ It's my grandmother's birthday. She's going to be 70. We're spending the weekend with her.

Your friend,

Laurel

2 Read the email again. Answer the questions. Write complete sentences.

1. What phrase does Laurel use to thank Adriana for the invitation?

   Thanks for inviting me

2. What phrases does Laurel use to apologize?

   _____

   _____

3. What is Laurel's reason for not going?

   _____

   _____

4. What suggestion does Laurel make at the end?

   _____

   _____

5. What two places does Laurel apologize in?

   _____

   _____

3 Write sentences to refuse an invitation to go to the beach. Use phrases from Exercises 1 and 2.

A: Can you come to the beach on Saturday?

1. Thank the person for the invitation:

B: _____

   _____

2. Apologize and refuse:

B: _____

   _____

3. Explain why you can't go:

B: _____

   _____

4. Suggest another time:

B: _____

   _____

10 Have Fun!

VOCABULARY Free-time activities

1 Complete the free-time activity phrases.

celebrate	✓play
go	play
hang out	read
have	spend
listen	take

1. _____play_____ video games

2. _____ photos

3. _____ a party

4. _____ your birthday

5. _____ books

6. _____ with friends

7. _____ time with your family

8. _____ an instrument

9. _____ to music

10. _____ to a dance

2 Complete the paragraphs. Use the verbs from Exercise 1.

1. When you ___celebrate___ your birthday, you _____ with your family, like your grandparents and cousins. You eat cake and open presents. Your parents always _____ photos when you blow out the candles on the cake.

2. My favorite things to do when I _____ with friends? That's easy. We like to _____ video games. We can play them for hours. And we often _____ to music, too.

3. My brother is very friendly. He doesn't like to spend time alone. His favorite thing to do is _____ to a dance at school. If my parents would let him, he'd _____ a dance party at our house!

4. My friend Carol is very quiet and spends a lot of time alone. She likes to _____ books. She also likes to _____ instruments. She is learning to play the drums. Maybe she won't be quiet any more!

3 Complete the chart with the activities from Exercise 1 and your own information. Then write sentences.

Activity	When?	Where?	Who?
1. hang out with friends	last weekend	sports park	Bill, Lisa
2. spend time with family			
3. celebrate birthday			
4. _____ _____			
5. _____ _____			

1. _I hung out with my friends Bill and Lisa last weekend. We went to the sports park._

2. _____

_____

_____

3. _____

_____

_____

4. _____

_____

_____

5. _____

_____

GRAMMAR Indefinite pronouns

1 Label the graphs with indefinite pronouns.

anyone	no one
anything	nothing
anywhere	nowhere
✓everyone	someone
everything	something
everywhere	somewhere

PEOPLE

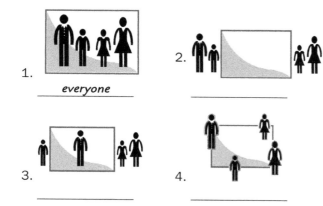

1. _everyone_

2. _____

3. _____

4. _____

PLACES

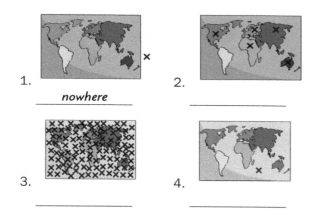

1. _nowhere_

2. _____

3. _____

4. _____

THINGS

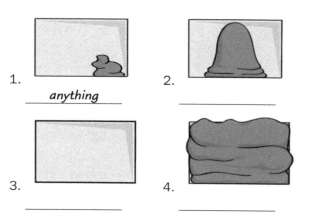

1. _anything_

2. _____

3. _____

4. _____

2 Complete the sentences with indefinite pronouns.

anyone	everywhere
anything	No one
✓everything	something

1. The food was delicious. He's eaten ____everything____ on his plate.

2. It's polite to bring _____ when you are invited to dinner.

3. Don't speak if you don't have _____ nice to say.

4. He can't remember _____'s name.

5. His passport is full of stamps because he's traveled _____.

6. _____ answered the last question correctly.

3 Correct the negative sentences. Mark ✓ if the sentence is correct.

anywhere
1. I didn't go ~~nowhere~~ fun on my birthday. _____

2. He didn't know no one at the party. _____

3. I don't know someone who loves football more than me. _____

4. Julie didn't do everything exciting on vacation. _____

5. Everyone goes to the free concerts in the park. _____

6. There is always anything to do at the city center. _____

VOCABULARY Adjectives of feeling

1 Use the pictures to complete the crossword.

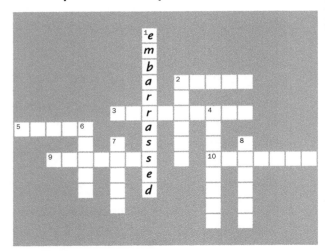

ACROSS

2. _____

3. _____

5. _____

9. _____

10. _____

DOWN

1. *embarrassed*

2. _____

4. _____

6. _____

7. _____

8. _____

2 Choose the correct words.

Scott: Hi, Ernie! Tell me about your camping trip with your brother.

Ernie: It was my first time camping. So I was ¹**embarrassed /** ⟨**excited**⟩ I guess I was also a little ²**nervous / upset** because anything could be out there in the woods, you know?

Scott: You're ³**scared / tired** of bears, aren't you?

Ernie: Yes! I am very ⁴**afraid / bored** of them. So, anyway, I was in my tent about to fall asleep, and I heard a noise outside. It was coming closer. My heart started beating very fast. I felt ⁵**embarrassed / stressed**. After a minute, I peeked out of the tent.

Scott: What was there?

Ernie: Something furry landed in front of my tent! I screamed. Then I heard my brother laughing. He threw his furry hat in front of the tent to scare me!

Scott: You must have really been ⁶**excited / surprised**.

Ernie: For a moment I was. Then my brother said he was ⁷**bored / nervous**, so he thought it would be fun to scare me. That made me ⁸**afraid / angry**. Then I was ⁹**embarrassed / surprised** that I screamed because the people in the next campsite heard me. And then I was ¹⁰**nervous / upset** with my brother for teasing me. I couldn't sleep all night. Now, I'm just ¹¹**scared / tired**.

Scott: That's kind of a funny story, you know.

Ernie: *Now* it is!

GRAMMAR *too and enough*

1 Circle the correct words to complete the rules.

1. Use **enough /** ~~**too + adjective**~~ **/**
   infinitive + infinitive to show something is more
   than what we want or need.

2. Use **adjective + enough + infinitive /**
   infinitive + enough / too + infinitive to show
   something is what we want or need.

3. ***Not + adjective / Not enough / Too + adjective***
   shows something is less than or more than what
   we want or need.

2 Complete the chart with *too* and *enough*.

	More than	What we want	Less than
tall	*too tall*	*tall enough*	*not tall enough*
warm			
brave			
nervous			
young			

3 Put the words in the correct order to make sentences.

1. ending / The / enough / wasn't / movie's /
   surprising / .

   The movie's ending wasn't surprising enough.

2. to / race / the / Bill / enough / wasn't /
   win / fast / .

   _____

   _____

3. home / was / sick / stay / Becky /
   enough / to / .

   _____

   _____

4. wasn't / He / nervous / too / to / remember /
   the / answer / .

   _____

   _____

5. it / They / talk / too / were / to / upset /
   about / .

   _____

   _____

6. spider / too / speak / was / when / he / Bob /
   saw / to / the / scared / .

   _____

   _____

4 Circle the correct words.

1. The boy is ~~**too short**~~ **/ n't short enough** to ride
   the bike.

2. He was **too afraid / n't afraid enough** to answer
   the door.

3. The team was **too strong / n't strong enough** to
   win the game.

4. She was **too tired / n't tired enough** to finish
   her homework.

5. The tea is **too hot / n't hot enough** to drink. You
   might burn your mouth.

5 Complete the sentences with your own information.

1. I'm (not) old enough to _____ *drive a car* _____ .

2. I'm (not) too scared to _____

   _____ .

3. I'm (not) brave enough to _____

   _____ .

4. I'm (not) interested enough to _____

   _____ .

5. Climbing a mountain is (not) something I'm

   _____ .

6. Acting in a movie is (not) something I'm

   _____ .

1 Match the suggestions with the responses.

1. Why don't we try surfing?

2. I want to see the new zombie movie.

3. Why don't we go shopping?

4. How about watching the skateboarders?

5. Why don't we go swimming?

6. How about calling our friends to join us?

a. That's a great idea! Luckily, I brought my bathing suit.

b. I'd rather watch the surfers. They're more exciting.

c. I'm too scared to try that. I'd rather go swimming.

d. That's a great idea! I heard it's really good.

e. That's a great idea! You call Jorge, and I'll call Kaitlin.

f. I'd rather be outside than in a mall. Maybe we can do that tonight.

2 Choose the correct suggestion or response.

1. **A:** Why don't we go see that new horror movie?
   B: I don't like horror movies. **That's a great idea! / I'd rather see the new action movie.**

2. **A:** It's a nice day. How about we go for a walk?
   B: **I'd rather go for a walk. / That's a great idea!**

3. **A:** We haven't seen our cousins in a while. **How about we stay home? / Why don't we visit them?**
   B: That's a great idea!

3 Complete the conversations with your own ideas. Use the phrases in the box.

| How about | That's a great idea |
| I'd rather | Why don't we |

1. **A:** Let's go skiing.
   B: It's too cold. _Why don't we go to the movies?_

2. **A:** _____ go skiing?
   B: There's not enough snow.
   _____
   _____

3. **A:** _____ playing video games?
   B: It's too nice outside.
   _____
   _____

4. **A:** _____ studying for the test this afternoon?
   B: _____
   _____

5. **A:** _____ go to the museum?
   B: _____
   _____

1 Read the email and complete the chart.

```
○○○
📄 📁 ✈ 📎 🗑
    To  Raquel
  From  Paul
Subject  Let's go power-kiting!
```

Hey Raquel,

How are you? I saw your windsurfing photos online. There were some good ones!

I'm having a party this weekend, and you're invited. It's a party to introduce my friends to the sport of power-kiting. It's like skateboarding with a kite. We're going to try it at the park. I don't know if you've tried power-kiting before, but I think you'll like it because you like wind sports. I tried it last weekend, and it is easier than it looks.

We'll meet at the skate park at noon on Saturday. Then after we power-kite for a couple hours, we'll go to Rocky's for pizza. If you can't join us for power-kiting, you can meet us there.

Let me know by Thursday if you can join us. I need to let the park know by then how many people are coming.

Your friend,

Paul

Paul's Party	
1. What is the event?	*power-kiting party*
2. What is the reason for the event?	
3. When is the event?	
4. Where is the event?	
5. What are the activities?	
6. What response does Paul ask for?	

2 Read the email again. Underline the referencing words *ones*, *it*, *there*, and *then*. Then draw a line from the referencing word to the noun it refers to.

3 Complete the sentences with the correct reference words.

1. I have a lot of good friends. I have a lot of fun with _____*them*_____.

2. Why don't we go downtown on Saturday afternoon? Are you free _____?

3. How about coming to the concert with me tonight? I think you'll really like _____.

4. Are you learning to play the guitar? How is _____ going?

5. Why don't we spend some time with your cousins? I really like hanging out with _____.

6. I would like to go to the movie with you tomorrow, but I'm busy _____.

1 Look at the pictures. Circle the correct answers.

Ken: I fell playing ice hockey last winter, and I ¹**broke / fell off** my ²**ankle / shoulder**. Then I couldn't walk. While it was healing, I sat on the sofa a lot and ³**went dancing / spent time with my family**. They gave me a camera so I wouldn't be ⁴**bored / nervous**. That's when I started to ⁵**play an instrument / take photos**. I was ⁶**stressed / surprised** how much I liked it.

Emma: I love to ⁷**celebrate my birthday / read books**. This year, we had a big party at my house. There were candles on the cake, and they ⁸**burned / sprained** the paper on one of my gifts! I ate too much cake, and my ⁹**elbow broke / stomach hurt**. It was fun to ¹⁰**have a party / play video games**, but I was ¹¹**stressed / tired** afterwards.

Roger: Last summer, I was mountain biking, and I ¹²**crashed / sprained**. I ¹³**fell off / hurt** and ¹⁴**banged / slipped** my knee. I couldn't walk for a while. I thought I would play video games, but my mom said I should ¹⁵**have a party / play an instrument**. That's why I started to learn the guitar.

2 Match the actions with the feelings.

1. Jackie slipped on the floor in the cafeteria.
2. Bill fell asleep in school.
3. Pam didn't like playing video games.
4. Alex played the violin in his first concert.
5. Anna had to read a lot of books for her test.

a. He was nervous.
b. She was bored.
c. She was embarrassed.
d. She was stressed.
e. He was tired.

3 Circle the correct answers.

1. Have you ever broken a toe?
   a. Yes, she has.
   b. No, I haven't.
2. What bones have you broken?
   a. Yes, I have.
   b. My arm and a finger.
3. Has he ever gone power-kiting?
   a. Yes, he has.
   b. He slipped yesterday.
4. What happened when Mike fell off his bike?
   a. He sprained his arm.
   b. No, he hasn't.
5. Have they ever lost a game?
   a. Yes. They lost one last week.
   b. Yes, I have.

4 Circle the correct answers.

1. I don't see any_____ to buy in this store.
   a. -one   b. -thing   c. -where
2. I've looked every_____ for the cat.
   a. -one   b. -thing   c. -where
3. I don't think any_____ could surf those waves.
   a. -one   b. -thing   c. -where
4. There's _____ who can come on Saturday.
   a. anyone   b. everyone   c. no one

5 **Write questions and answers with the present perfect or the simple past.**

1. Millie / crash her bike / ever (yes, last month)

   Q: _____

   A: _____

2. Paula / go kite-surfing / before (no, power-kiting)

   Q: _____

   A: _____

3. Stefan / live Madrid / ever (no, Buenos Aires, last year)

   Q: _____

   A: _____

4. You / study English / ever (yes, two years ago)

   Q: _____

   A: _____

6 **Rewrite the sentences to make them correct.**

1. Tom didn't tell no one about the surprise party.

   _____

2. Why have he be late for school every day this week?

   _____

   _____

3. Cara hasn't broke any bones before.

   _____

4. Sam slip at the pool yesterday.

   _____

7 **Complete the emails with the correct phrases.**

haven't been	sounded like fun
How about	That's a great idea!
I'd rather	Too bad
I'm too scared	Why don't you

```
O O O
📄 📁 ◁ 📎 🗑
     To  | Dylan
   From  | Lena
Subject  | RE: Invitation
```

Hi Dylan,

How are you? Thanks for the invitation to go swimming last weekend. I was out of town. We went surfing in Sayulita. Sorry I missed it. It ¹_____.

I'm taking a group of friends sky-diving next weekend. ²_____ coming along? It's not real sky-diving, like jumping out of a plane. It's indoors! You float in the air in a big wind tunnel. It looks cool. I ³_____ sky-diving before. Have you? ⁴_____ join us?

Let me know by Friday if you can make it.

Talk to you later,

Lena

```
O O O
📄 📁 ◁ 📎 🗑
     To  | Lena
   From  | Dylan
Subject  | RE: RE: Invitation
```

Hey Lena,

Indoor sky-diving? ⁵_____ ⁶_____ it's the same day as my cousin's birthday party. We're going to a car race. ⁷_____ try sky-diving than go to the race, but only because it's indoors. ⁸_____ to jump out of a plane. But thanks for inviting me.

Maybe we can go skateboarding on Sunday.

See ya!

Dylan

Carpets of DAGESTAN

BEFORE YOU WATCH

1 Look at the pictures from the video. Complete the sentences with the correct words.

business	carpets	colors	wool

It takes months to make these beautiful _____. These men work for a carpet _____ in Russia. They buy the _____ from sheep farmers and dye it different _____.

WHILE YOU WATCH

2 Watch the video. Are the sentences true (*T*) or false (*F*)? Correct the false sentences.

1. Dagestan is in southern Russia.   _____

2. Khan has a car business.   _____

3. He buys wool from his wife's sister.   _____

4. Khan's business makes 250 carpets a year.   _____

5. It takes four months to make a carpet.   _____

3 Watch the video again. Circle the words you hear.

1. People here speak over **30 / 40** languages.

2. He gives work to many **villages / villagers.**

3. The water can't be too hot or too **cool / cold**.

4. Only **men / women** make Khan's carpets.

5. In the evening, many women work on their **homes / farms**.

AFTER YOU WATCH

4 Work with a partner. Take turns saying what you have in your backpack. Where do the items come from?

I have a water bottle. It comes from China.

A Very INDIAN WEDDING

BEFORE YOU WATCH

1 **Look at the pictures from the video and read the sentences. Match the words with the definitions.**

Traditional Indian weddings are often big and beautiful.

Women paint the bride's hands with henna before the wedding.

The bride gives the groom rice during the wedding.

1. wedding _____   a. a woman who is going to be married

2. bride _____   b. a special paint

3. henna _____   c. a marriage ceremony

4. groom _____   d. a man who is going to be married

WHILE YOU WATCH

2 **Watch the video. Number the sentences 1–5 in the order you see them.**

1. The groom rides a white horse.   _____

2. The bride's family dances for her.   _____

3. Fifty people work on the flowers.   _____

4. The women draw henna on the bride's hands.   _____

5. The bride gives the groom rice.   _____

3 **Watch the video again. Check (✔) the sentences you hear.**

1. ❏ Some traditions are hundreds of years old.

2. ❏ People say red henna is a good sign.

3. ❏ They all prepare for the big day.

4. ❏ The groom is waiting.

5. ❏ They walk together today and for life.

AFTER YOU WATCH

4 **Work with a partner. Make a list of wedding traditions in your country.**

1. bride: white dress	4. music
2. groom: dark suit	5. flowers
3. wedding rings	

A Life on BROADWAY

BEFORE YOU WATCH

1 Look at the pictures from the video. Do you think the sentences are true (*T*) or false (*F*)?

1. In a musical, the actors sing and dance. _____

2. In most musicals, dogs sing. _____

3. There are many different kinds of jobs in the theater. _____

WHILE YOU WATCH

2 Watch the video. Circle the correct answers.

1. The star of the play is _____ years old.

    a. 10   b. 11   c. 12

2. The director tells the actresses _____ to move.

    a. where   b. who   c. what

3. The set designer creates the _____.

    a. play   b. lights   c. place

4. People prepare for _____ to put on a play.

    a. weeks   b. months   c. years

3 Watch the video again. Match the adjectives with the nouns you hear.

1. theater _____
2. popular _____
3. lighting _____
4. special _____

a. effects
b. designer
c. musical
d. capital

AFTER YOU WATCH

4 Work with a small group. Complete the chart below. Then discuss: What are some of your favorite plays or movies? Who were the actors? What parts did they play?

Movie / Play	Actor	Part	Actor	Part
X-Men	Hugh Jackman	Wolverine	Jennifer Lawrence	Mystique

> I really liked the new *X-Men* movie. Hugh Jackman was in it. He played Wolverine. Jennifer Lawrence played Mystique.

MUMBAI: *From* COMPUTERS *to* FILM

BEFORE YOU WATCH

1 **Look at the pictures from the video. Circle the correct answers.**

1. These people work **on farms / in offices** in Mumbai, India.

2. People make thousands of **films / computers** in Mumbai.

WHILE YOU WATCH

2 **Watch the video. Number the places and things 1–5 in the order you see them.**

1. a festival   _____

2. a bus   _____

3. a park   _____

4. Mumbai at night   _____

5. a train   _____

3 **Watch the video again. Are the sentences true (*T*) or false (*F*)? Correct the false sentences.**

1. Mumbai is a rich city.   _____

2. Ten years ago, the population of Mumbai was 20 million.   _____

3. Many people work in modern offices.   _____

4. Traditions are not important here.   _____

5. Some traditional festivals are part of India's film industry. _____

AFTER YOU WATCH

4 **Work with a partner. Discuss: What TV shows or movies take place in a big city? What do you learn about the city?**

Spiderman takes place in New York City. There are a lot of really big buildings . . . and a lot of people and cars.

Unusual FUN

BEFORE YOU WATCH

1 Look at the picture from the video. Check (✔) the sentences you think are probably true.

Mall of the Emirates

1. ❑ The mall has over 1,000 shops.

2. ❑ There are about 50 cinemas here.

3. ❑ You can ride bikes through the mall.

4. ❑ You can go skiing here.

WHILE YOU WATCH

2 Watch the video. What are people doing in the mall? Write short answers to the questions.

1. Are some people ice skating? _____No, they aren't._____

2. Are some people snowboarding? _____

3. Is a little girl holding a balloon? _____

4. Are the boys looking at skis in the store? _____

5. Do the boys buy sunglasses? _____

3 Watch the video again. Circle the correct answers.

1. Dubai is in the United Arab **States / Emirates**.

2. It's often about **40 / 45** degrees Celsius here.

3. The mall has **120 / 125** restaurants.

4. The mall is in the middle of the **Arabian / Sahara** Desert.

5. A lot of kids come here to **eat / have fun** with their friends.

AFTER YOU WATCH

4 Work in small groups. Discuss the question at the end of the video: Is there a mall near you? What fun things can you do there? Where do you like to shop?

Yes, there is. I like going to movies there . . . and I like visiting the electronics store.

ZERO: PAST *and* PRESENT

BEFORE YOU WATCH

1 Look at the pictures from the video. Complete the sentences with the correct numbers.

| 0 | 2 | 10 |

1. We use the ancient Indian system of _____ digits: 0–9.

2. The number _____ represents nothing, or no quantity.

3. In ancient India, people used the same word for *arms* and for the number _____.

WHILE YOU WATCH

2 Watch the video. Check (✔) the sentences you hear.

1. ❏ From nothing – or zero – came everything.

2. ❏ These ancients used numbers, not words, for quantities.

3. ❏ So, around 11 B.C.E., they invented symbols.

4. ❏ We use numbers with zero and nine.

5. ❏ Think about zero the next time you go shopping.

3 Watch the video again. Complete the sentences with the correct words.

1. The word *digit* comes from the Latin word for _____.

2. We have _____ numbers in our system.

3. Can you imagine life without _____?

4. In computing, there are _____ digits.

5. Prices usually contain _____.

AFTER YOU WATCH

4 Work with a partner. Complete the chart with your information. Then read it to your partner, who will write the information using words, not numbers.

Time	I slept for _____ hours and _____ minutes last night.
Weight	My backpack weighs about _____ kilos.
Price	A new laptop costs about _____ pesos.
Speed	An airplane flies at about _____ kilometers an hour.

Wildlife HERO

BEFORE YOU WATCH

1 Look at the pictures from the video. Complete the sentences with the correct words.

| in danger | rhino | wildlife | vet |

1. Animals that live in nature are called
   _____.

2. A _____ is a doctor who takes care
   of animals.

3. A _____ is a large animal with
   thick skin.

4. Some animals are not safe. There are only
   a few of them in the world.
   They are _____.

WHILE YOU WATCH

2 Watch the video. Number the animals 1–5 in the order you see them.

1. A giraffe in a truck _____

2. Two zebras drinking water _____

3. A rhino running in a field _____

4. A lion opening its mouth _____

5. Two elephants playing _____

3 Watch the video again. Match the phrases to make true sentences.

1. Yanna wants the animals to _____

2. Yanna's job is dangerous because _____

3. Yanna is going to _____

4. At first, the sedative _____

5. Yanna does this job because _____

a. the black rhino is in danger.

b. take the rhino to a new home.

c. the animals are wild.

d. be safe from hunters.

e. makes the rhino fall asleep.

AFTER YOU WATCH

4 Work in a small group. Discuss: Have you, or has someone you know, ever saved an animal? What happened?

> My brother and I once found a kitten. We took it home. We gave it food and water.

The Chilean MINE RESCUE

BEFORE YOU WATCH

1 Look at the picture from the video. Match the words from the video with the definitions.

1. drill _____   a. to save someone from danger

2. miner _____   b. a safe place

3. refuge _____   c. a machine that makes holes

4. rescue _____   d. a person who works in a mine, deep underground

WHILE YOU WATCH

2 Watch the video. Are the sentences true (*T*) or false (*F*)? Correct the false sentences.

1. In 2010, there was a terrible accident in Chile.   _____

2. There were 32 men in the mine.   _____

3. The rescue workers found the miners seven days after the accident.   _____

4. The miners wrote a note to the rescuers.   _____

3 Watch the video again. Circle the correct answers.

1. What happened when the giant rock fell?

   a. It killed many miners.   b. It closed the exit to the mine.   c. It made a deep hole.

2. The rescuers gave the miners a _____.

   a. drill   b. TV   c. phone

3. The men were in the mine for more than _____ months.

   a. two   b. three   c. four

4. How many people watched the final rescue of the miners?

   a. two billion   b. one million   c. one billion

AFTER YOU WATCH

4 Work with a partner. Discuss: Imagine you are trapped inside a mine. What do you feel? Say? How do you keep calm?

> I feel afraid. I'm really worried. I tell my friends that people will save us. I try to breathe deeply.

Mysteries in the
MOUNTAINS

BEFORE YOU WATCH

1 Look at the picture from the video and read the story. Then match the words and the definitions.

Archaeologists study ancient civilizations. They ask questions: Who were these people? How did they live? Some archaeologists were working in Bolivia when they found bones. They looked at the bones with a microscope. They were the bones of a young woman . . .

1. archaeologist _____

2. civilization _____

3. bones _____

4. microscope _____

a. the hard, white pieces that form the frame of a human or animal body

b. a tool that makes small things look bigger

c. a scientist who studies ancient cultures

d. a culture; a society

WHILE YOU WATCH

2 Watch the video. Are the sentences (*T*) or false (*F*)? Correct the false sentences.

1. Last year, Scotty went to Tiwanaku. _____

2. He was studying an ancient culture. _____

3. The archaeologists found bones and hair. _____

4. They found corn next to the bones. _____

5. The Tiwanaku people grew lots of corn. _____

3 Watch the video again. Circle the words you hear.

1. They look for clues and **answer / answers** to questions.

2. They lived here in the mountains about **a thousand / two thousand** years ago.

3. The bones were strong and the teeth were **heavy / healthy**.

4. He wanted to look at it **closely / carefully** under a microscope.

5. So, this woman wasn't **from / of** here!

AFTER YOU WATCH

4 Work in a small group. Discuss: Do you like reading about mysteries or watching mysteries on TV? What are some of your favorites?

> I like *Paper Towns* by John Green . . . and *Buzz Kill* was a great book. I always watch *Pretty Little Liars* – it's amazing!

The Case of the MISSING WOMAN

BEFORE YOU WATCH

Unit 5 Video 5.3

1 Use the clues and the words to complete the crossword puzzle.

disappear interview missing remember search worry

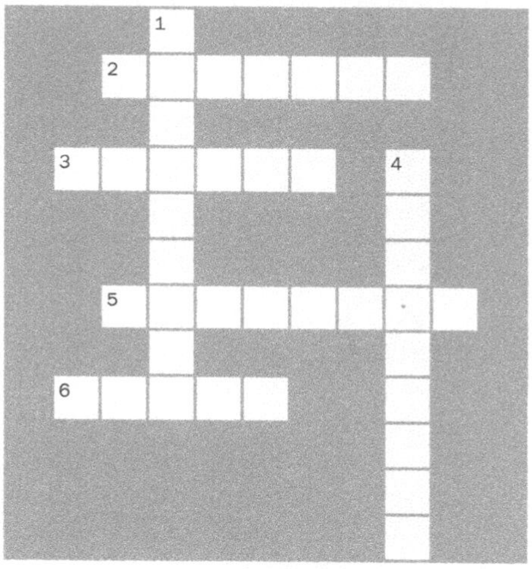

ACROSS

2. not there, absent
3. to look for
5. to think of someone or something from the past
6. to feel nervous or anxious

DOWN

1. to leave; to go out of sight
4. to ask someone questions, get information

WHILE YOU WATCH

2 Watch the video. Number the sentences 1–5 in the order you see them.

1. The police found Amber's car. _____
2. A video camera showed Amber in a shop. _____
3. The police interviewed Amber's family and friends. _____
4. The police found a woman in a park. _____
5. Amber's car keys were missing. _____

3 Watch the video again. Match the sequencing words you hear with the events.

1. One day, _____
2. Soon _____
3. Two days ago, _____
4. Then _____
5. Finally, _____

a. Amber was safe.
b. police found a woman in a park.
c. Amber disappeared from her hometown.
d. the police found the next clue.
e. Amber was inside the shop alone.

AFTER YOU WATCH

4 Work with a partner. Think of a mystery (a book, a TV show, or a movie) you both know. Take turns describing what happened.

A: In *Veronica Mars*, Veronica has an interview in New York City.
B: Then her boyfriend calls her.
A: Right. So she returns to Neptune . . .

A Cool LIFE

BEFORE YOU WATCH

1 **Look at the picture from the video. Circle the correct words to complete the sentences.**

1. This house in Coober Pedy, Australia, is **underground / above ground**.

2. When it is very hot outside, it is **cooler / warmer** in this house.

3. This house needs a lot of **lamps / bedrooms**.

WHILE YOU WATCH

2 **Watch the video. Number the sentences 1–5 in the order you see them.**

1. Two people walk into a mine.   _____

2. People play golf outside at night.   _____

3. A woman cooks in her kitchen.   _____

4. A woman finds an opal in a mine.   _____

5. A man cleans his living room.   _____

3 **Watch the video again. Look carefully at the rooms in the underground house. Check (✔) what you see, and where.**

Object	Living room	Dining room / Kitchen	Bedroom
lamps			
pictures			
beds			
table			
chairs			

AFTER YOU WATCH

4 **Work with a partner. What do you do when it is really hot or cold outside – during the day or at night?**

> When it's really hot, I swim during the day. At night I read. When it's very cold, I go ice skating during the day. At night, I watch TV.

Moving HOUSE

BEFORE YOU WATCH

1 Look at the picture from the video and read the text. Then match the words with the definitions.

Joey was looking for a new house. He found a cabin he liked. He put the cabin on logs. He used a bulldozer to pull the cabin to a new place.

1. cabin _____   a. a big machine that can move things

2. log _____   b. a small wooden house

3. bulldozer _____   c. a thick piece of a tree

WHILE YOU WATCH

2 Watch the video. Circle the correct answers.

1. Joey lives in the _____ of Tanana, Alaska.

   a. city   b. town   c. state

2. He lived with his father until _____ ago.

   a. a month   b. a year   c. two years

3. He doesn't have _____ money.

   a. much   b. more   c. some

4. He wanted to live _____ his family and friends.

   a. with   b. next to   c. closer to

5. Joey's _____ move the logs.

   a. brothers   b. cousins   c. friends

3 Watch the video again. Check (✔) the sentences you hear.

1. ❏ Can he buy the house and move?

2. ❏ So first, they must get some logs.

3. ❏ It's really hard work.

4. ❏ I'm very excited!

5. ❏ It's perfect!

AFTER YOU WATCH

4 Work with a partner. Take turns describing your favorite room at home. What does it look like? What do you like to do in it?

> My bedroom is my favorite room. There's a bed and two windows . . . and my computer. I like listening to music in my bedroom.

A *Pizza* ROBOT

BEFORE YOU WATCH

1 **Look at the picture from the video. Find the words in the puzzle.**

customer	deliver	order	pizza	robot

B	O	R	L	C	N	F	R	A	Z
P	I	C	U	S	T	O	M	E	R
A	E	Q	Z	S	P	I	Z	Z	A
R	O	B	O	T	O	T	A	C	I
A	F	R	D	O	X	Z	F	U	B
S	D	H	V	M	K	Z	X	A	O
P	E	J	D	E	L	I	V	E	R
O	R	D	E	R	A	P	B	R	O

WHILE YOU WATCH

2 **Watch the video. Circle the correct answers.**

1. The men work on _____ in the US.

   a. a lake   b. a river   c. an island

2. The pizza from the blimp is _____.

   a. cold   b. hot   c. delicious

3. One of the men in the robot car is _____.

   a. driving the car   b. watching a video   c. using a computer

4. The men put _____ on the smaller robot.

   a. glasses   b. clothes   c. a sign

5. One man opens Luigi's _____ with a credit card.

   a. oven   b. box   c. window

3 **Watch the video again. Complete the sentences with the correct words.**

itself	map	problems	ready	without

1. A robot car drives _____.

2. The car has _____ at first.

3. In the future, robots will use a city _____.

4. Luigi goes around the car _____ a problem.

5. They get a hot pizza _____ to eat.

AFTER YOU WATCH

4 **Work with a partner. Discuss: What do you think robots will do for people in the future? Make a list, and then share it with another pair.**

> **A:** I think robots will clean houses in the future.
>
> **B:** I think they'll cook dinner.

Music SHARING

BEFORE YOU WATCH

1 **Look at the picture from the video. Complete the paragraph with the correct words.**

download	industry	sharing	store

Twenty years ago, people had to buy music from a music ¹_____. Then it became possible to ²_____ music files on a computer. This changed the music ³_____. Will file ⁴_____ be illegal in the future?

WHILE YOU WATCH

2 **Watch the video. Are the sentences true (*T*) or false (*F*)? Correct the false sentences.**

1. In 1999, it wasn't easy to get music. _____

2. Shawn Fanning created a computer to download songs. _____

3. Soon Napster became a big business. _____

4. Bands got money from Napster for their music. _____

5. Record companies stopped file sharing. _____

3 **Watch the video again. Complete the sentences with the words you hear.**

1. What part will music _____?

2. In one _____, more than 10,000 people had it.

3. Soon a million _____ had it.

4. So they closed Napster _____.

5. Maybe you will have the _____ big idea!

AFTER YOU WATCH

4 **Work in small groups. Discuss: What do people buy online, and what do they buy in a store?**

> My parents buy books and DVDs online. They buy food at a store.

A School at HOME

BEFORE YOU WATCH

1 Look at the pictures from the video. Read the definition. Do you think the sentences are true (*T*) or false (*F*)?

homeschool (verb) to teach your children at home

1. Children in many countries are homeschooled. _____

2. Very few homeschooled students attend a college or university. _____

3. Many homeschooled students are active in their communities. _____

4. Homeschooled students usually learn about only one subject. _____

WHILE YOU WATCH

2 Watch the video. Circle the correct answers.

1. Maggy's **mother / father** helps her on the computer.

2. Her **mother / father** teaches classes at home.

3. The Botros children study science, English, and **math / history**.

4. Maggy **would / wouldn't** like to go to a large school.

5. Maggy wants to be a **teacher / scientist** in the future.

3 Watch the video again. Match the phrases to make true sentences.

1. My oldest son has _____   a. work out for him.

2. School just didn't _____   b. away from home.

3. Maggy is really _____   c. some special needs.

4. Sometimes Maggy studies _____   d. close to her brothers and sisters.

AFTER YOU WATCH

4 Work with a partner. Compare your school to the school in the video. What do you like best about each type of school?

> My class is bigger than the class in the video. I like the small classes in the video. I really like playing soccer at my school.

Time for an
ADVENTURE!

1 **Look at the pictures from the video. Match the words with the correct defnitions.**

1. chef _____

2. archaeologist _____

3. dinosaur _____

4. volunteer _____

a. an animal that lived on Earth millions of years ago

b. a professional cook

c. someone who chooses to help or do work without getting paid

d. a scientist who studies ancient cultures

WHILE YOU WATCH

2 **Watch the video. Check (✔) the sentences you hear.**

1. ❑ So I'm taking a year on after high school.

2. ❑ Perhaps I'll go to Siena and work as a volunteer.

3. ❑ It has wide, open spaces and green forests.

4. ❑ Or I'll visit a village and see people my age.

5. ❑ Maybe I'll help an archaeologist look for a T-Rex!

3 **Watch the video again. Match the adventures with the places.**

1. Rome _____

2. Siena _____

3. South Africa _____

4. Madagascar _____

a. repair old buildings

b. look for dinosaur bones

c. learn to cook

d. help animals

AFTER YOU WATCH

4 **Work in small groups. Discuss: What adventures are you going to have when you finish school?**

> I'm going to go hiking in the mountains for a week . . . and I'm going to college in a big city. That will be an adventure.

DANGER *in our* FOOD

BEFORE YOU WATCH

1 Look at the pictures from the video. Do you think the sentences are true (*T*) or false (*F*)?

1. Many people become sick every year from eating bad food. _____

2. Food that will make you sick usually looks delicious. _____

3. Water in public places is always safe to drink. _____

4. Fruits and vegetables are safer to eat than cookies. _____

WHILE YOU WATCH

2 Watch the video. Complete the sentences with the correct words.

1. Madison was like many _____.

2. Sometimes there is E. coli in food and _____.

3. The _____ are worried.

4. The E. coli was in the _____dough.

5. _____ was very lucky.

3 Watch the video again. Check (✓) the sentences you hear.

1. ❑ She enjoyed dancing and singing with her friends.

2. ❑ E. coli 0157 is a kind of bacteria.

3. ❑ How did Madison get E. coli?

4. ❑ The doctors taste many different kinds of food.

5. ❑ Soon over 70 people are ill with E. coli.

AFTER YOU WATCH

4 Work in small groups. Discuss: Have you or a family member ever eaten something that made you really sick? What did you eat? What did you feel like?

> I ate some fish a year ago and got really sick. I felt sick to my stomach. I didn't want to eat anything for days.

A DEADLY *Job*

BEFORE YOU WATCH

1 Look at the pictures from the video. Label the pictures with the correct words. Then answer the questions.

| crocodile | kangaroo | snake | spider |

1. _____ 2. _____ 3. _____ 4. _____

5. Which of these animals are dangerous? _____

6. Which of these animals sometimes live in people's homes? _____

WHILE YOU WATCH

2 Watch the video. Number the snakes 1–5 in the order you see them.

1. a snake in a pantry   _____

2. a snake on a rock   _____

3. a snake in a bag   _____

4. a snake in a box   _____

5. a snake on the floor of a room _____

3 Watch the video again. Circle the correct answers.

1. Adelaide is on the **south / north** coast of Australia.

2. The brown snake is the **most / second most** dangerous snake in the world.

3. Snake-Away takes snakes **to / from** people's homes.

4. The man must hold the snake by its **head / tail**.

AFTER YOU WATCH

4 Work with a partner. What animals or insects live in people's houses? Which are dangerous?
Complete the chart.

Animal	Dangerous?
Cat	No
Dog	Sometimes
Ant	

A New York City
FOOD TOUR

BEFORE YOU WATCH

1 Look at the pictures from the video. Complete the sentences with the correct words.

delicatessen	desserts	hot dogs

1. New York City has food from all over the world. You can get a delicious lunch in a _____ like this one.

2. People sell _____ and sandwiches on the streets of New York.

3. Some places only serve _____, like this ice cream sundae.

WHILE YOU WATCH

2 Watch the video. Circle the correct answers.

1. Katz's Delicatessen is the _____ in New York.

    a. largest   b. oldest   c. busiest

2. Sylvia's Restaurant opened in _____.

    a. 1888   b. 1952   c. 1962

3. People go to Serendipity to eat _____.

    a. desserts   b. hot dogs   c. pizza

4. The fudge that people eat at Serendipity is made of _____.

    a. ice   b. cream   c. chocolate

3 Watch the video again. Number the sentences 1–4 in the order you see them.

1. A man in a red T-shirt dancing   _____

2. A woman with big earrings eating a sandwich   _____

3. A man in a black T-shirt cutting meat   _____

4. A group of horses crossing a street   _____

AFTER YOU WATCH

4 Where can you go to get great food where you live? Complete the chart below. Share your list with a partner.

For . . .	Place	Great food
Lunch	Rosetta	seafood tacos
Dinner		
Dessert		

Punkin CHUNKIN!

BEFORE YOU WATCH

1 Read the definitions of the words from the video. Then find the words in the puzzle.

pumpkin (noun) a large, round, orange vegetable

chuck (verb) to throw

launch (verb) to send something into the air

shoot (verb) to cause something to fly or move quickly; to use a gun

U	M	P	O	P	R	L	C
I	A	L	A	U	N	C	H
X	H	W	P	M	Q	Z	S
T	S	H	Z	P	R	E	T
C	H	U	C	K	F	D	O
B	O	A	V	I	H	V	M
H	O	I	N	N	J	O	E
E	T	H	O	T	R	R	R

WHILE YOU WATCH

2 Watch the video. Are the sentences true (*T*) or false (*F*)? Correct the false sentences.

1. Everyone calls this sport a mess.

2. People build machines to chuck the pumpkins. _____

3. People come here every two years for this festival. _____

4. Jake works so hard because of his family. _____

5. Jake's father was the world champion. _____

3 Watch the video again. Check (✓) the sentences you hear.

1. ❑ Have you heard about the Punkin Chunkin contest?

2. ❑ Some people say it's a sport.

3. ❑ So why do people do this?

4. ❑ Now the whole family helps shoot pumpkins!

5. ❑ To chuck pumpkins, why else?

AFTER YOU WATCH

4 Work in small groups. Discuss: What are some unusual traditions in your town or country? Does your family have any unusual traditions?

> My family has an unusual tradition for New Year's Eve. At midnight, we break dishes in the kitchen. Then we go outside to plant a tree!

Notes

Credits

The authors and publishers acknowledge the following sources of copyright material and are grateful for the permissions granted. While every effort has been made, it has not always been possible to identify the sources of all the material used, or to trace all copyright holders. If any omissions are brought to our notice, we will be happy to include the appropriate acknowledgements on reprinting.

p.3 (TL): Shutterstock Images/Sergiyn; p.5 (TR): Alamy/©The Photolibrary Wales/Steve Benbow; p. 10 (1): Getty Images/Steve Granitz/WireImage; p. 10 (2): Getty Images/Sonja Flemming/CBS; p. 10 (3): Alamy/©ZUMA Press; p. 10 (4): Getty Images/Steve MORT/AFP; p. 10 (5): Getty Images/Jasin Boland/NBC/NBCU Photo Bank; p. 10 (6): Getty Images/Alexander Tamargo; p. 10 (7): Alamy/©Jochen Tack; p. 10 (8): Alamy/©Pictorial Press Ltd; p. 10 (9): Alamy/©AF archive; p. 11 (TL): Alamy/©Blend Images/Jeff Greenough; p. 14 (CL): Shutterstock Images/FXQuadro; p. 18 (CL): Alamy/©Daniel Dempster Photography; p. 27 (TL): Alamy/©Everett Collection Inc; p. 33 (TR): Alamy/©Megapress; p. 37 (CR): Alamy/©Andreas Von Einsiedel; p. 39 (TL): Shutterstock Images/Julian Rovagnati; p. 47 (TL): Shutterstock Images/Ermolaev Alexander; p. 50 (1): Alamy/©MBI; p. 50 (2): Getty Images/Jupiterimages; p. 50 (3): Shutterstock Images/Michaeljung; p. 50 (4): Shutterstock Images/Pierdelune; p. 50 (5): Getty Images/MachineHeadz; p. 50 (6): Shutterstock Images/Denis Kukareko; p. 50 (7): Alamy/©Jim West; p. 50 (8): Shutterstock Images/oliveromg; p. 50 (9): Alamy/©age fotostock Spain, S.L.; p. 50 (10): Shutterstock Images/Sofia Andreevna; p. 51 (BL): Alamy/©Andres Rodriguez; p.53 (BL): Shutterstock Images/Mariyana M; p.53 (BC): Alamy/©Oote Boe 3; p. 56 (1): Shutterstock Images/Africa Studio; p. 56 (2): Shutterstock Images/Roadk; p. 56 (3): Shutterstock Images/Photosync; p. 56 (4): Shutterstock Images/Veronchick84; p. 56 (5): Shutterstock Images/Stephen Mcsweeny; p. 56 (6): Shutterstock Images/Africa Studio; p. 56 (7): Shutterstock Images/R.Legosyn; p. 56 (8): Shutterstock Images/Kellie L.Folkerts; p. 56 (9): Shutterstock Images/Liu Anlin; p. 56 (10): Shutterstock Images/MichaelJay Berlin; p. 56 (11): Getty Images/Wavebreak Media; p. 59 (CL): Shutterstock Images/PhotoSky; p. 63 (TR): Alamy/©Purcell Team; p. 64 (BL): Getty Images/Tim Hall; Back cover: Shutterstock Images/Vibrant Image Studio.

Front cover photograph by Alamy/©Marc Hill.

The publishers are grateful to the following illustrators:

Janet Allinger p. 6, 32, 54; Galia Bernstein p. 19, 25, 26, 31, 40, 41, 45, 55, 66 (TR), 67, 70; Anni Betts p. 2, 21, 28, 30, 60, 61, 68; Alberto de Hoyos p. 22 (1-5, 7, 9, 10), 58 (1-10); Nigel Dobbyn p. 4, 8, 48, 52 (TR), 62; Mark Duffin p. 44 (1-3, 5-7); Simon Ecob p. 9, 14, 15, 17, 24, 35; Q2A Media Services, Inc. p. 7, 19, 25, 26, 31, 40, 41, 44 (4), 45, 46, 52 (TL), 55, 65, 66, 67, 70; Jose Rubio p. 12, 13, 20, 22 (6, CR), 34, 42, 43, 58 (C); David Shephard p. 36; Norbert Sipos p. 38, 49.

All video stills by kind permission of Discovery Communications, LLC 2015.